GREAT COST-CUTTING IDEAS

FROM LEADING COMPANIES AROUND THE WORLD

Anne Hawkins

Marshall Cavendish
Business

Copyright © 2010 Anne Hawkins

Cover art: Opal Works Co. Ltd.

First published in 2010 by Marshall Cavendish Business
An imprint of Marshall Cavendish International

PO Box 65829
London EC1P 1NY
United Kingdom
and
1 New Industrial Road, Singapore 536196
genrefsales@sg.marshallcavendish.com
www.marshallcavendish.com/genref

Other Marshall Cavendish offices: Marshall Cavendish International (Asia) Private Limited, 1 New Industrial Road, Singapore 536196 • Marshall Cavendish Corporation. 99 White Plains Road, Tarrytown NY 10591-9001, USA • Marshall Cavendish International (Thailand) Co Ltd. 253 Asoke, 12th Flr, Sukhumvit 21 Road, Klongtoey Nua, Wattana, Bangkok 10110, Thailand • Marshall Cavendish (Malaysia) Sdn Bhd, Times Subang, Lot 46, Subang Hi-Tech Industrial Park, Batu Tiga, 40000 Shah Alam, Selangor Darul Ehsan, Malaysia

Marshall Cavendish is a trademark of Times Publishing Limited

The right of Anne Hawkins to be identified as the author of this work has been asserted by her in accordance with the Copyright, Designs and Patents Act 1988.

A CIP record for this book is available from the British Library

ISBN 978-981-4276-92-4

Printed and bound in Great Britain by
TJ International Limited, Padstow, Cornwall

CONTENTS

Acknowledgments

My thanks go to the members of Cheltenham Connect Skillspace for their support and contributions, and in particular to Belinda Wilson (GlosJobs.co.uk); Pia Cato (Vanilla Pod Bakery); Jonathan Pollinger (Intranet Future); Mike Reed (REEL Solutions); Jonathan Moffitt (Auditel); Anthony Salloum (Comsal) and Karen Wilson (Colour Matters Decorating and Interiors).

Neil Radbourne and Adrian Hughes are also to be thanked for their contribution of ideas. Others enthusiastic to share their experiences – but understandably unwilling to disclose their identities – include Trevor, Paul, Andy, Lesley, Steve, Stephanie, Brian, Jeremy and Jacqueline.

Last, but by no means least, my thanks to my husband Steve, without whose tales of trials and tribulations this book would not have been possible.

Anne Hawkins

INTRODUCTION

WHY ARE YOU reading this book?

Don't get me wrong, I'm delighted you're doing so.

But I hope you haven't picked it up expecting to find 100 great ideas all about how to slash the amount you spend.

Is that all you're looking for?

Aren't you really interested in improving your profit and, more importantly, your profitability? (If you work for a charity or another not-for-profit organisation, don't worry, this book is also for you. After all, you're just as interested in making every £1 you can raise achieve as much as possible, so there's plenty in here for you as well.)

You see, there is a difference in scope.

If you restrict yourself to just finding ways to reduce your costs, you overlook the opportunity to use the costs you do incur more effectively to increase your sales and thereby improve your bottom line. So I'd politely suggest it's not really costs you're interested in as such, it's improving your profit.

And please don't stop there.

If you were offered the opportunity to invest in a business that guaranteed you a profit of £1,000 this year, would you be interested? Anything else you might want to know before making up your mind? Besides the obvious matters of risk and legality there is the key question of how much you have to invest to earn that profit. If you had to invest £10,000 you could well be interested. If you had to invest £1m you would walk away. So actually what really matters to you is not how much profit you make but how much profit you make relative to how much had to be invested to earn that profit – i.e. profitability.

So I suspect we've now established that it's not just improving your profit that you're interested in, it's really profitability. Take a look at IDEA 34 for an explanation of how you go about improving your profitability and the opportunities for tapping into the multiplier effect.

And while I'm at it, I may as well point out that many profitable businesses go into liquidation because they run out of cash. Really? (If you're not sure about how this can happen take a look at IDEA 44.) Perhaps you'd also like some ideas on how to keep cash flowing into the business so that you're around long enough to enjoy your profits?

It might be helpful at this stage to point out a few not-so-great ideas.

Anxious to improve the financial performance of his division, this manager took me to one side and asked, "Do you think if I account for my costs in a different way my products will be more profitable?" I gently pointed out that if he managed his costs better and/or improved his sales, his products would become more profitable. After all, it's not about how you cut the cake… it's the size of the cake you're cutting.

Lured by the apparent savings to be made by sub-contracting work, this other business, unable to do anything with the released capacity, ended up paying not only their own business costs but also those of their supplier. (This one's actually worthy of further thought. Although it results in increasing your costs in the short-term, it might not be quite so daft as it sounds. Intrigued? You might like to start with IDEA 89.)

Beware the 'quick fix' where, with sleight of hand, your costs improve only to reappear as soon as your back's turned. Using rogue consultants to help you take stock out of your business can be a great example of this (see IDEA 96). Look for root causes and come up with proper 'fixes' – don't just put out the fire, take away the matches.

You see, when it comes down to it there are only 3 ways to improve the financial performance of your business:

- reduce the costs you incur while maintaining the amount you sell

- increase the amount you sell without proportionately increasing your costs

- reduce the amount of investment needed to do the same amount of business

So here are 100 ideas to get you started.

THE IDEAS

THE IDEAS ARE garnered from personal experience, straightforward good business practice and from a range of contacts in a wide spectrum of businesses (from multinationals to sole traders), with the emphasis on practical steps you can take.

While the intention is that you dip into the book for inspiration, links are provided to help you thread your way through the ideas should you want more about particular themes.

The ideas could be grouped into 5 loose categories:

Power in numbers
While you may strike lucky and find ideas you can lift directly from the book and implement in your business, the key to unlocking great improvements in your business is really beyond you.

Or at least it's beyond you alone. Do you have a passive, silent majority under your roof? All too often gung-ho managers busy themselves with 'improvements' without spotting what often proves to be the greatest source of the greatest ideas there before their very eyes... the rest of the workforce. Which is why some of the ideas are about how to switch on and engage everyone in the continuous hunt for finding even better ways for doing more with less. You could start with IDEA 91.

Managing the basics
There's nothing cost-effective about managing a brood of headless chickens.

You need to agree on your vision for the business before turning your attention to how you're going to get there. Once that's sorted, you can then begin to make plans for the first stage of the journey, and thence to the budgeting process in which you allocate your scarce resources to the achievement of each part of that short-term plan.

And it doesn't stop there. Don't just carry on walking regardless without checking the map, your watch and the condition of your hiking boots. Find out how you're doing and monitor how much it's cost you to get there. After all, you can only manage if you measure. If you want to embark on this journey you could board at IDEA 7.

Starting at the top

This is not a book about sales techniques. There are plenty of good books available about those – including another title in this series. But it is a book about cost improvement and you don't just improve your costs by cutting them. The significance of the impact of incremental business often gets overlooked – if you can use the costs you're incurring in your business to generate more revenue, then that's great for your bottom line too. Better still are the ways you can take your top-line improvement straight to the bottom line – IDEA 66 will get you thinking.

People, materials and services

It's possible that your payroll costs are not the biggest spend in the business, but your people are likely to be your most important investment. Don't employ people for them to just spend their time dropping £50 notes into the shredding machine (see IDEA 90).

The only difference between suppliers and employees is the way in which you pay them, so choose your partners with care (see IDEA 18). What you buy, how much you buy, who you buy from and how much you pay will all impact your business costs. As will how much you use. Cost improvement is not about getting better prices, it's about getting better value.

Putting the squeeze on investment

When it comes down to it, what you're really after is not profit, but profitability.

(If you've got any doubts, go back and take a look at the Introduction.)

There's no point improving your costs in order to make shed-loads of profit if you've tied up so much money in the process that you're making a lousy return on your investment. Take a look at the explanation of the difference between profit and cash in IDEA 44 to start you thinking about the levers you have to pull to turn those profits into cash, then move on to look at some of the other great ideas for how to squeeze value out of your investment.

This book is not intended to be a step-by-step guide on how to revolutionise the improvement in financial performance of your business. It is, however, designed to provoke your thoughts.

Your business is unique.

It has its own problems and hence its own opportunities. You should find that some of the ideas strike a chord and you will be able to see almost immediately how they could be used in your business. Others may have an underlying message that can be interpreted and adapted to suit the challenges you are facing. There may be some you set aside – for now.

If, as you dip into the ideas, you feel a sense of growing excitement that there is no end to the possibilities for improvement, and an eagerness to start putting your ideas into practice, then the book will have fulfilled its purpose.

So where are you going to start?

A DROP IN THE OCEAN

JUST LIKE OTHER utility bills, you need to monitor and manage your water bill.

Do your meter readings make sense?

Check the serial number on the meter – does it match the one on your bill?

Check where the meter has been fitted. There are plenty of horror stories out there of people finding they have been paying not just for their own water but those of their neighbours... and even the leak in the pipe that was not their responsibility.

The idea

Even if you've checked that you've been billed correctly, you can't manage the cost of water if you don't know where it is being used.

Envirowise* claims that businesses can save around 30% of their water costs through implementing simple and inexpensive water minimisation measures such as fixing dripping taps and installing water-saving devices.

Bring it home

Encourage everyone to question the quality and the quantity of the water being used and look for opportunities to save. You may find that people with unmetered water supplies at home are less water-aware than those used to watching how much money they pour (or flush) down the drain. Losing mains water for several weeks as I did and having to carry water from an erratically-filled bowser stationed some distance away down the road (while not recommended), can literally bring it home just how much water you use.

Keep checking
Read your meter on a regular basis so that you pick up on and investigate abnormal usage (e.g. from a leaking pipe) in a timely manner.

Quality costs
Remember that you usually get charged twice – once for the water supplied and then again to have it taken away.

Could you use alternatives to mains water?

How about using rainwater or reusing grey water?

Measure how much water is being used for different purposes and then start thinking of ways to reduce usage.

Flush out savings
You will be using water in your restrooms. While you may not want to follow Australian guidance**, if you work out approximately how many restroom visits are made by your total workforce in a day you might decide to reconsider the way water is used there. Sensors on urinals and tap aerators are just some of the ideas that can generate substantial savings with rapid paybacks in these areas.

Where else do you use water in your business?

- Cleaning vehicles?
- Washing components?
- Office cleaning?
- In the canteen?
- Watering plants?

What about the water you drink?

Water water everywhere...

Opinions vary on how much water humans need a day – whatever the amount, there's no need for it to cost you an arm and a leg...

Looking through the pile of suggestions made by employees, this one caught the manager's eye – and his imagination. It was suggested that plastic cups for use at water-coolers could be eliminated by providing everyone with a water-bottle. This started him thinking. Everywhere you looked there was a water-cooler. People seemed to believe they needed cooled water at arm's length wherever they went.

Rather than using expensive bottled water, coolers are now connected to the mains wherever possible. By removing half the coolers on site, the company has saved £10,000 per year in contract charges. (The manager commented that after a few days of anger and frustration, people realised that having a short walk to get their water wasn't such a bad thing as it gave them the opportunity for a bit of exercise and allowed then to stretch their stiff bodies.) And once they are at the water machine they now fill up their water bottles rather than using plastic cups – even better!

[Even if you're not too keen on the water-bottle idea, consider the size of the cups you use. If they're too big, people just pour away tepid remains (water that you've paid for and paid to chill) and refill again with more water that you've paid for...]

Of course with cost improvement there's always something more to do. This particular client achieved some stunning cost improvements in recent years in many different aspects of the business. Yet when I went into the cloakroom, I noticed the hot tap was running. When I walked over to turn it off and found that I couldn't a friendly voice called over, "Don't worry, it's been like that for ages..." When you consider that one dripping tap can cost more than £900 per year in water and waste treatment charges* (and this was hot water)... there was an awful lot of money going down that drain.

In practice

- Treat water as a valuable commodity.

- Take a look at each water-consuming activity you carry out in your business and considering how you would re-engineer it if you had to carry the water from a well 5 miles away.

- Check your invoices!

* Source: Envirowise website March 2010 www.envirowise.gov.uk. Envirowise is a UK resource efficiency programme funded by Defra in England, Scottish Government in Scotland, the Materials Action Programme in Wales and Invest Northern Ireland. From April 2010, an integrated Resource Efficiency Programme will be led by WRAP in England. This programme will embody many of the proven Envirowise services and information contained in the Envirowise website.

** If it's yellow, let it mellow. If it's brown, flush it down.

2 A FRESH SET OF EYES

THE NEW MANAGER watched in disbelief as the operator took the component out of a box, threw away the box, attached a part to the component and then re-packaged it in a new box identical to the one he'd just thrown away.

As soon as you hear the words "That's how we do it here", you should sniff the possibility of cost improvement. For all too often, an unquestioning continuation of processes and procedures without any real understanding of why the task is required can throw up opportunities for eliminating waste.

The idea

When looking for improvements, bring in new blood from a different part of the business. People without preconceptions who have no qualms in asking over and over again that simple, but often profound question, "Why?" (see IDEA 27)

(On training courses those who preface their interjections with, "This is probably a dumb question but..." almost inevitably initiate great discussions on really fundamental issues.)

Multiple benefits

Not only do multi-disciplinary teams increase the probability that the status quo will be challenged, they also bring other advantages.

By involving people from different areas of the business, there can be cross-fertilisation of ideas as improvements suggested for one area can be replicated elsewhere, thereby engaging a multiplier effect.

Gaining an understanding of other aspects of the business is part of personal development and can also help people identify inter-departmental waste (see IDEA 57).

Sometimes that fresh pair of eyes can save a fortune.

Documented overkill

One of the major customers of this components manufacturer complained that the product he received was out of specification. As a result, he insisted that all the products supplied to him should come accompanied by extensive documentation covering the inspection of key dimensions, together with assembly and test information.

This time-consuming and expensive procedure was put in place as a short-term fix to overcome a specific quality problem.

The company then chose to extend the procedure to every product that went through the same process. And then extend it to every product that went through the factory. The sales team, seeing the opportunity to differentiate their product, would then offer to supply this documentation, free of charge, to every new customer and every new part.

Wind the clock forward 15 years. Yes, 15 years.

The components manufacturer no longer had a quality problem and no longer even made the products that caused this documentation process to be initiated. But the documentation packs continued to be produced. What was supposed to be a 'quick-fix' to overcome a short-term problem had become ingrained in company procedure.

And it didn't stop there.

Because of the complexity of the documentation it was difficult to keep up-to-date with, for example, revisions to drawing issue numbers and changes to assembly and test methods. So the company started to fail quality audits because of discrepancies between products to be shipped and this pack of 'supporting' but totally superfluous 'information'. And as a consequence of failing audits, more training took place and even more documentation was prepared...

All it took was for one person to ask, "Why are we doing this...?"

In practice

- Build teams from across the organisation wherever practicable.

- Initiate discussions on processes and procedures not with the question. "How do we do this?" but rather with the question, "Why do we do this?"

3 | A HEALTHY BOTTOM LINE

You've identified the skills you need from your workforce, you've recruited and trained them so that's sorted.

Not if they're not there.

Holidays you understand and can plan for. But what about absenteeism? This is not a cost to be sneezed at.

The idea

You check your payroll for 'ghost-workers' to make sure payments are only going to genuine employees. But even they may not be visible...

Someone for nothing

If you employ 100 people and you have 6% absenteeism, it is the equivalent of 6 people on your payroll never showing up for work. Put another way, if you could reduce that rate to 2% then that's equivalent to having 4 extra people for free – or 4 vacancies you will not have to fill. And if your payroll costs are 50% of your total costs, then your costs could fall by 2%.

Could a 2% reduction in cost double your profit (see IDEA 91)?

The cost of absenteeism doesn't stop at wasted payroll costs. Even if the person isn't there, the work is. If output isn't to suffer other people must rush around to cover the work, causing additional costs (see IDEA 22). But do they have the necessary skills? (see IDEA 77) Resentment builds and they too become tempted to 'pull sickies' and the virus spreads.

Induced sickness

Absenteeism can be rife in some organisations. A colleague recently recounted that when he started work he was taken to one side by one of his peers for a short 'unofficial' induction process. Included in the other insights into the business culture was the advice that, "You have 4 weeks holiday and 2 weeks sick leave on top of that. Don't go and show everyone else up by not taking your full entitlement."

Firm but fair

An enterprise, renowned as a caring employer, reviewed their performance statistics and decided that enough was enough.

They set about tackling their unacceptable rate of absenteeism in a positive manner by demonstrating great support to genuine cases – but a firm hand with malingerers who prefer to 'swing the lead'.

The first step was to monitor and analyse absenteeism and try to identify the cause of the problem. Patterns of behaviour emerged. Younger employees were often absent around the weekend. Those with school-age children were more likely to be 'ill' during school holidays. Some would repeatedly be 'off sick' just before or after time booked off for holidays. It was time to act. The message was:

"This matters"

Employees were made aware absenteeism was under the spotlight and that incidences of absence would be one of the matters discussed at the newly-introduced individual annual appraisal system.

"We care"

Back-to-work interviews with supervisors were introduced to discuss and record the reason for absence. If the person has been unwell they will be asked if they have gone to the doctor and if they are now fit enough to return to work. The employee is asked whether they are on medication and if so, whether there are possible side-effects that might be important to matters of health and safety.

In preparing for the interview, supervisors will have looked through the records of a person's previous absences to take appropriate action. For example, if there are recurring incidences of flu they might recommend checking with the doctor about a vaccination.

Those on long-term sick leave are visited by their supervisors rather than someone from HR, unless there is a suggestion that the supervisor has contributed to the reason for the absence. Because they know the person better, the supervisor is more likely to be able to gauge just how serious the illness is.

For both recurring short-term absenteeism and longer-term absence where there is real cause for concern for the employee's health and it is felt that there is insufficient support being provided by the state-funded system, the company will pay for private consultations.

"We will take action"

Where there is proof of abuse, disciplinary action is taken. In recounting his story, the manager added that it only took a couple of official warnings for the message to get through that the company would not tolerate unwarranted absence. (An unexpected consequence was the level of 'grassing' that took place from those employees who for years had deeply resented the additional workloads they had had to carry because of their colleagues' malingering.)

With absenteeism having dropped by 5% to 2%, these strategies are paying off.

In practice

- Check your rate of absenteeism and analyse the incidences. (Even if it's low overall there may be pockets of localised infections.)

- Develop your own action plan for ensuring your workforce is fit for purpose!

A POWERFUL ARGUMENT

ENERGY MAY BE one of your business' biggest single spends.

But do you know where and when you use power?

Do you use this information to negotiate the best deals?

How do you monitor and control your usage to use your spend most effectively?

The idea

You can't begin to manage without information.

Get your supplier to provide you with a web page of what you're using and when. Find out where your electricity is being used either by getting in a contractor to monitor equipment (who will typically do the work for 50% of the resultant savings), or buying the kit to do it yourself.

Lights out
(This is not about working unmanned shifts – although that in itself might be a great idea – but about what goes on after dark.)

It may surprise you just how much power you are using when you've locked up and gone home. Identify where this power is being used and develop procedures to turn things off where practicable. (e.g. Even if the IT department wants systems left on for maintenance you should still make sure monitors are turned off.) If you think your meter is still going round faster than it should, it's worth investigating...

During a power-cut, this cinema switched on their generator and were surprised to find that in so doing they also turned on the streetlights for a significant stretch of the road outside. How many years had they been paying for this?

While you're at it, check out your water meter – a surprising number are incorrectly fitted and you may be paying for someone else's use (see IDEA 1).

Losing heat

Are you using power to generate heat and then wasting it – or even worse, then using air-conditioning to keep everyone cool?

In the factory – do you run equipment such as degreasers at the right temperature, and are the lids closed when they are not in use?

In the kitchen – you probably pay the bills so are catering contractors incentivised to manage energy usage?

Compressed air – did you know that 95% of the energy used in running compressors may be lost as heat? (see IDEA 79)

Too much control

You may be wasting energy with systems fighting each other for more control than you really need.

Not only were the heating system and the chilling system in this particular temperature-controlled environment continually battling each other, the situation was exacerbated by the tolerances being much more tightly specified than were actually necessary.

In another clean room, the air was being continually changed to the highest specification – even when the factory was shut down for the weekend.

New Equipment

As part of the approvals process for buying new equipment, is consideration given to energy efficiency?

Factory Maintenance

Well-maintained buildings are likely to be far more energy efficient. Get help to do the sums on the impact of improved insulation, etc. If your building can't have cavity wall insulation you could be losing up to 35% of your heat through the walls. Don't give up – there are insulating paints available that claim to reduce this loss by 25%.

In practice

- Collect information on how much power you use and what it's used for.

- Look at each type of use for ways to eliminate waste.

- Continually review your pattern of usage and the deals around to negotiate the best package.

- There may be opportunities to re-schedule your usage to improve your costs (see IDEA 48).

5 A QUESTION OF RESPECT

How MANY PEOPLE are employed by your business?

How many of them play an active role in challenging the status quo and looking for better ways to do more with less?

The idea

When you set out on the improvement journey there may be some 'low hanging fruit' (obvious, easy quick-fixes), where benefits can be derived by a select group of individuals who may well have become experts in appropriate tools and techniques.

But are there even better solutions?

Are there more pressing problems – and hence opportunities?

What do you tackle next?

Sadly, many businesses fail to use the talents, knowledge and abilities of a large proportion of the workforce who often know all too well how and why things go wrong, but for one reason or another do not feel it is appropriate to speak out.

If you need to change your business culture to gain momentum in improvement activities, understand the issues.

There may be general disengagement.

Disinterest
If your invitation to others to join in improvement activities are greeted by mumblings of "It's not my job to tell you how we could do

things better. I just do what I'm told", then you may need to roll up your sleeves and explain the harsh realities of life. (A more persuasive approach might be adopted by those who have read IDEA 91.)

However, the barrier to active participation in suggesting improvements could be, as with this international business, a cultural disinclination to question or challenge.

Respect differences

Pleased with the contributions being made by a significant proportion of his employees to improvement activities in the UK factory, this manager then turned his attention to the site in the Philippines. Here he found that while the workforce were hardworking and co-operative, individuals were reluctant to suggest ways to improve the instructions they had been given by a supervisor or manager about how to carry out their work.

It was a question of respect. Only when a framework was developed – within which individuals could put forward ideas without compromising cultural norms – did the suggestions for improvements start to flow. Employee exchanges between the two sites also helped reinforce the message that making suggestions for improvements wasn't just acceptable – it was a key part of their job!

In practice

- Look objectively at your business and measure the proportion of people who not only understand that their contributions matter, but who are also actively involved in improvement activities.

  Not enough?

- Tackle this by making everyone aware of the benefits of a team-approach (see IDEA 91), then spot your 'carriers' (see IDEA 51) and get to work on them!

6 A RISKY BUSINESS

INVENTORY IS LIKE a hot potato – pass it on as quickly as possible to the next person down the line not just because it ties up unnecessary investment (see IDEA 37), but because holding it also increases the risk of your fingers getting burnt. And your money.

The idea

Drive down your lead-time through the business, because if it exceeds the time the customer is prepared to wait for their order, you're going to have to hold inventory to keep your customer satisfied.

All inventory not contractually covered by a customer order is a risk to the business (and even if you do have order cover, you're at risk if the customer's business fails!).

If you have to scrap inventory off because it no longer has any value to the company, the cost has to be written off against profit.

Too much!
It will help to keep an eagle eye on your inventory and try to make sure you use up the items you already have on the shelf (see IDEA 36).

Standardising designs can also contribute to reducing risk as common parts reduce the likelihood of obsolescence (see IDEA 46).

Design changes (whether driven by quality problems, a break-through in technology... or the whims of designers) can result in products and components gathering dust on the shelf.

Moving markets

The longer inventory takes to work its way through the business, the more likely you are to get caught out if the market changes.

Changes to the market can be fashion-driven. Retailing is fraught with the challenges of fashion-conscious customers, particularly if you are appealing to the 'trend-setter' market.

In the clothing industry, unseasonable climatic changes can cause problems.

Adverse or favourable publicity – either about the company or the product – can influence the rate at which your products fly off the shelf. Your market can disappear completely if your only customer stops trading.

But the key driver to the extent of these risks is time.

Time is money

The shorter the total lead-time through the business, the less inventory you will have caught in the system that you could be unable to invoice and turn into cash.

(Remember that 'time' starts ticking from the moment you make a contractual commitment to a supplier, and continues right through to when the customer takes ownership. If your customer requires you to hold inventory on consignment – whether on or off your premises – the clock continues to tick until the trigger point to invoice him for the items he's taken.)

Do you understand how much risk you're running? It's worth checking – or, even better, writing something into – the contractual small print.

The victim of downward revisions to customer schedules, this business was caught with substantial inventory on their books. At first sight it looked a devastating blow. On careful examination of the contractual small print, however, they managed to negotiate a substantial recovery to the costs they had incurred as the contract wording was successfully argued to have effectively committed the customer to 'buying' a given production capacity.

Quick off the mark
Of course, shortening lead times not only reduces the risk you're carrying, but also has the upside of enabling you to respond quicker to opportunities to grab additional business – whether due to a general upturn in the market or being able to take advantage of a competitor's problems.

In practice

- Understand your risk exposure and attack the time your business ends up holding inventory on its books.

- Question the need to hold inventory on consignment for your customers. The requirement may date back to a time when your delivery performance was poor and these things have a habit of getting ingrained in working practices (see IDEA 2). And with the consignment inventory as a free of charge 'buffer', the customer is unlikely to raise the matter for you.

- Reflect on how, before you take on business, you might be able to mitigate some of the risk of holding inventory by charging a booking fee or negotiating cancellation charges or progress payments.

- Talk to your designers to make sure they understand the impact their design choices have on how much inventory you hold and how long you have to hold it for (see IDEA 97), and therefore the risk they bring to the business.

- Remember that even when the customer has been invoiced, you're still at risk until he pays (see IDEA 28).

A SHARED VISION

Do YOU AND your colleagues have the same vision for where the business is going?

Do you share this vision with everyone who works for you?

Do you set performance measures that are consistent with this vision?

If people choose for themselves the grid reference towards which the company is heading and use different maps for the journey, you're going to be wasting valuable resources.

If, however, you have a shared vision you can use this to coordinate efforts and direct resources to the activities that need to take place to get you to where you want to be.

The idea

Take the time and space required to develop and agree on the vision for your business.

You need everyone to refocus attention from day-to-day matters (where 'long-term planning' might take you to the end of the week) to looking to the future. So get your team away from the coalface and use an outsider as facilitator if you think this would help.

Re-group
If you've agreed where you're going, don't do things that aren't in the plan – at least not before you've consulted your colleagues.

If opportunities arise that hadn't been considered when setting the vision, you might need to reconvene and rework the process.

Failure to keep working together and pulling the business in the same direction will be costly as individuals head off in pursuit of their own goals. Where there's friction in a machine you lose energy in unwanted heat. Where there's friction in a business there's cost and lost potential.

A fork in the road

The product of a management buyout, this service provider, headed by its two energetic owner-managers who had worked together for years, flourished.

As time passed, however, tensions grew and it became evident that the managers had quite different visions of where the future of the business lay.

With such a shared history there was a reluctance to face the issue full on and instead, for a while, the business lurched along as a result of decisions being taken on a piecemeal basis rather than in line with an agreed strategy. Eventually, unable to ignore their differences any longer, the managers went their separate ways and have continued journeying successfully – but along divergent routes and towards different horizons.

Consistent messages – and measures

Once you've agreed on your vision you can then decide what needs to be achieved in specific timeframes and set top-level performance measures to enable you to mark your progress. These top-level measures should then be cascaded down as individual 'metrics' to everyone in the organisation so that they take ownership of their contribution to the overall plan.

For instance, if one of the top-level measures were to increase profit-to-cash conversion from 70% to 80%, the most significant contribution most people could make would be to take actions that would result in the reduction of the investment in Working Capital.

The storekeeper's metrics might therefore include measures of the time taken between receipt of goods and their availability for issue from stores and the accuracy of his inventory records.

If another of the top-level measures were to reduce inventory write-offs from say, 5% to 2%, the storekeeper's contribution may be to improve the rotation of stock and he would be measured accordingly (see IDEA 10).

In practice

- Make sure you and your whole team share the same vision of where the business is going.

- Establish a pyramid of cascading metrics to reflect the contribution everyone needs to make to achieve the dream and use these as an integral part of individual performance appraisals.

- Prepare budgets that are consistent with the resources required to achieve each part of the plan (see IDEA 69).

8 A TAXING QUESTION

FEW PEOPLE WANT to pay more tax than is necessary.

Tax takes away some of the business' hard-won profits (and more importantly cash) that you would have loved to keep for other purposes.

The idea

Always remember the important difference between tax avoidance and tax evasion. The first one is a legitimate activity carried out to minimise the cost of tax to the business. If you carry out the second one, you are likely to end up behind bars.

Minimising your liability to the taxman can be greatly aided by getting yourself a good accountant.

If you get it right you may well be able to more than cover the cost with savings in your tax bill – especially if you're constantly getting fined for late submissions and late payments.

Ask around. Get recommendations from others in a similar kind of business to you and operating on a similar scale – accountants tend to specialise.

Then negotiate.

While accountants may charge astonishingly high hourly rates, you can minimise your bill by making the work they're going to do for you as straightforward as possible.

Professional rates for professional work
Don't get caught for the cost of the accountant having to carry out the

duties required to salvage a situation he will kindly (but expensively) refer to as 'Incomplete Records'.

If there's clerical work to be done, pay a clerk – at a fraction of the amount your accountant will charge you.

This creative entrepreneur pays an accountant to prepare her accounts. Having recently dropped a large box full of assorted paperwork on her accountant's desk she light-heartedly related how her accountant had gone pale and protested that 'this wasn't included in the agreed fee'.

How pale will the entrepreneur's face be when she sees her accountant's bill?

You could start by...

- Being organised. Agree with your accountant (or your auditors) what records you're going to keep and the format in which you're going to keep them.

  Then do it.

9 AN OFFER YOU CAN'T ACCEPT

If you're going to make an offer, make sure you understand the cost of its being accepted!

Pricing your products or services as 'offers' suggest lower revenue for the same cost. So what place does this have in a book of cost-improvement ideas?

Think again.

The idea

If you view offers as the cost to the business of reduced revenues you'll realise why they have to be planned, managed and controlled.

Every £1 you deduct from the selling price is £1 off the bottom line (profit).

It's all too easy to take the soft option to win business by cutting prices. Marginal (or incremental) costs are a lethal weapon in the hands of reckless commission-driven sales representatives – before you know where you are, all your business is marginal and nothing makes enough money to cover your business costs.

Challenge the purpose of any offer, and question the possible ramifications.

- To get rid of unwanted stock? – have you taken into account the impact on other product lines?

- To attract new customers? – if only new customers are eligible for the offer, how will it affect your relationship with your existing customers?

- To fill surplus capacity? – will customers expect such discounts to continue?

"Loss leaders" can have a place in your business strategy if you're convinced that the additional business they bring in (either immediately or, more uncertainly, in the future) will compensate you for the cost of that 'lost' revenue.

This doesn't always happen.

A not-so-tasty offer

A rather exclusive local restaurant decided to attract new customers by offering a substantially reduced price for a 3-course meal on Mondays when business was usually relatively quiet. Diners were seated at less attractive tables, presented with a fixed menu offering very little choice and therefore, given the restaurant's reputation, from the customer's viewpoint, a relatively poor experience. While overall the discounted meal represented reasonable value-for-money, diners left the restaurant somewhat disgruntled and unwilling to return.

A sign of poor management

A local store ran promotions that were for fixed time periods with pricing automated through the tills. Poor housekeeping resulted in offer signage being left on shelves after the expiry date. Goods requiring weighing were often not re-labelled when offers were introduced or ended. Given that the store promised to refund twice the difference should a customer be charged a higher price at the till than that shown on the shelves, the damage to the revenues (and hence the profits) was evident. Perhaps not many shoppers spotted the 'opportunities' for buying items at prices that were more of a bargain than intended. Perhaps the store was large enough to take the blow of this unnecessary cost... but perhaps your business isn't.

Don't put yourself in a position of unlimited liability. Set timescales for offers and clearly indicate expiry dates. Judging by the motley collection of valid coupons gathering dust on noticeboards and tucked into wallets, not all businesses are in a position to finally 'close the books' on the financial impact of offers – yet.

In practice

- Make sure there is a system in place to justify, monitor and control offers.

- Proposed offers should be signed-off not just by the sales manager but also by those who will be responsible for sufficient stock being available to meet demand and by those invoicing the customer.

- Have effective procedures in place for closing-off offers in relation to promotional materials, order-taking and invoicing.

- Keep a tight rein on the pricing activities of those in sales!

10 BE CAREFUL WHAT YOU WISH FOR!

You GET WHAT you measure – so make sure that what you measure is what you want.

The purpose of performance measures (often known as metrics or KPIs – Key Performance Indicators) is to select a small group of measures that will reveal not only how well the business is performing but also, when compared to targets, where there is need for improvement if plans are to be achieved.

It is important that the measures chosen are 'holistic' and that achieving them collectively will result in better overall business performance.

The idea

Don't single out individual metrics and improve them to the detriment of others.

Holistic health

Take the analogy of someone who decides to enter a marathon. It is sensible, when about to embark on an intensive fitness program (or an improvement regime), to go to the doctor for a check-up. Humans (like businesses) are a mass of complex processes or activities. Does the doctor (or should you) try to measure everything? No, he selects a few key measures such as blood pressure, cholesterol and body mass index to ascertain how fit our potential athlete is now and what areas he needs to work on to become even fitter (and hence more competitive) into the future. Just the same with businesses.

Let's assume the doctor tells our runner that the only thing that matters is weight-loss. At the next check-up our determined athlete has taken the doctor at his word and shed so much weight that he can hardly stand, let alone compete.

Similarly, if you tell people that the only thing that matters in the business is getting inventory levels down they'll come down.

But your customers will probably suffer.

If you tell the buyers the only thing that matters is making purchase price savings you'll get them.

But you may have to expand your stores (as a result of bulk buying), and buying cheaper items may not result in the overall cost-savings you had anticipated (see IDEA 49).

When setting measures of performance, it's important that they flow consistently from top-level objectives down to individual or team metrics and do not conflict!

Avoid mixed messages

Measured on their ability to bring in business, members of the sales team in this company spotted an opportunity to win a substantial amount of additional work if they could reduce the turnaround time on orders from the customer. It was decided that it was cost-effective to lay down additional inventory in order to achieve this. The inventory was purchased and the sales team advertised the reduced leadtime for orders and the extra business started to pour in.

As did the customer complaints when goods failed to be delivered as promised.

The reason? Nobody had talked to the team in the despatch department who were sitting on goods for several days before shipping them. Why? Because they were being measured on their performance in consolidating shipments to reduce carriage costs as part of a separate campaign to improve margins.

In practice

- Take a fresh look at where your business is going, what you need to do to achieve this, and therefore the measures you need to have in place to manage your progress (see IDEA 7).

- Make sure that your measures don't send out conflicting messages and that you get across the point that the objective is overall business performance improvement, not departmental gratification (see IDEAS 49 & 57).

BE RESOURCEFUL!

11

MAKE THE MOST of what you've got. If you use your materials more efficiently you'll also have less to dispose of – and in some instances that can be a costly business.

The idea

Getting value for money from your materials isn't just a question of the price you've paid for them. You need to minimise waste and look for cost-effective solutions to dispose of what's left. [Even if you've managed to obtain your materials free of charge (see below), you're going to want to use them as effectively as you can.]

Don't feed the skip

With expensive materials it can pay to invest to save. This business uses computer software to assist with bedding parts more effectively and, with laser cutters allowing parts to be positioned closer together, there is even less material in the off-cut bin.

With aluminium plate being more expensive than aluminium bar, this manufacturer switched from cutting parts out of plate to machining the shapes from bar on a CNC machine and then slicing the bar to size.

If you're using your materials more efficiently you'll also have less to dispose of – and in some instances that can be a costly business.

Finding a use for those slow-moving items in stores (see IDEA 36) will divert them away from their gradual progression towards the skip.

Reductions in the amount of scrap you produce (see IDEA 58) will also stop those skips filling quite so quickly.

Sell it on!

But despite everything you've done, you're almost inevitably left with materials and other items to get rid of.

Look creatively at how you could either sell unwanted items, or at least have them picked up and disposed of free of charge.

Make sure that there are procedures in place (and that they are adhered to) for segregating materials to maximise their value... and that your problem doesn't just disappear overnight (see IDEA 68)! Scrap metal can be valuable if sorted and stored appropriately.

Recycle

Make arrangements for free of charge collections for items that can be recycled; such as paper, plastic bottles and plastic coffee cups.

Site the recycling points appropriately and conveniently.

In the canteen, place recycling containers alongside collection points for trays so that everyone clears these items from trays as they finish their meals. This not only promotes recycling, but saves time for catering staff as trays can be stacked and cleared more efficiently. (Asking your diners to scrape their leftover food into receptacles for the local pig-farmers might prove a step too far for those with a delicate disposition... and an unwanted reminder of school dinners... although it might prove a useful motivator for reducing waste.)

Have a recycling point next to the coffee machine as you can track down contractors who will collect plastic coffee cups (and even pay you something for them) if they are slotted into a purpose-designed receptacle.

Don't have individual bins in offices but have central recycling points. Not only will this help you reduce your cost for garbage removal, but it should also help you make savings on your cleaning contract costs (see IDEA 67)!

Find your ideal partner.

There are agencies out there (including those funded by the government) desperate to match you with businesses who want your unwanted items – or, on the flipside, who could supply you with products you could use either at a knock-down price, or, in some instances for free. Successful 'marriages' might include using materials from demolished buildings for groundworks on new housing estates, using your 'rubbish' as a source of power or forming an alliance with a scrapstore. (Scrapstores typically collect tons of business waste each year at no cost to the donor and pass it on to groups to be used for art or educational purposes.)

In practice

- Look at the flow of materials and other products through your business.

- Consider whether there are cost improvement opportunities by re-engineering what you do to use someone else's waste.

- Question whether you use your resources as effectively as possible and whether for example, you re-use off-cuts whenever practicable.

- Find out how much you spend on waste collection. Delve through the skips and see what's in there... and then think creatively!

BE VIGILANT

ALL EXPENDITURE SHOULD be authorised.

Don't go over the top – convoluted authorisation procedures just tie up more of your time and money – but you do need to make sure there is a proper process for committing the company's money.

But even if you do have authorisation procedures in place, some types of expenditure have a habit of finding their way round the system and catching you out.

The idea

Make sure you don't end up paying for things you don't want or didn't have. Beware of:

Evergreens
These are those purchase agreements that automatically renew if you fail to take action. Companies rely on your disorganisation (or inertia) – and you'll end up paying for it. If you do decide to take on contracts set up in this way, make sure you immediately put an entry in your diary to review your needs (and shop around) well in advance of any trigger-dates. A chart of all such contracts can be a helpful visual reminder of when you need to take action. If you regularly price-check your motoring insurance you'll understand the kinds of savings to be made – either by changing supplier or by negotiating a matched price.

Scams
Don't be misled into paying for things you never ordered. A classic scam played particularly on small businesses is to invoice you for an

entry in a trade directory that you never authorised. Other common scams include receiving unsolicited faxes that appear to offer you great discounts on a product but you find that faxing back for further details costs you dearly.

Look out for invoices for renewing your domain name. Is the name right – look carefully. Is it renewal time? Did the invoice come from the same place as last time? Are payments to be made to the same bank account?

Incorrect pricing
If mistakes by utility companies and some supermarkets are anything to go by, there's loads of cost improvement opportunities here!

In practice

- Run off a report of all invoices paid without a purchase order reference as these will identify instances where the normal authorisation procedures have been bypassed.

- Chart any evergreens.

- Remind everyone of the importance of checking the small print – and if they're not authorised to sign or are uncertain as to what they're signing for – don't!

- Make sure people check the invoices they receive – and that goes for your bill from the taxman as well!

BUYER AWARE!

You've decided the exact specification of what you need – how do you make sure you're getting the best value for money?

How do you make the best use of every £1 in your budget?

Use your specialists in the purchasing department.

The idea

All non-payroll expenditure should go through the purchasing department, where there is expertise in identifying alternative sources of supply and negotiating the best deal (not just in respect of price but also with regard to payment terms).

Does this always happen in your business?

It can be very frustrating to find that the buyers have been avidly scrutinising every penny spent on materials and consumables and negotiating every bit of credit they can from suppliers only to find that new equipment has been ordered, costing thousands of pounds, without competitive quotes being requested or prices and payment terms negotiated.

(The argument that the buyers do not understand the required technical specification is not good enough. If the authorisation procedure is effective, the final selection will require the signature of the person who has responsibility for the investment to confirm it meets the required capabilities and the signature of the buyer to confirm the best deal has been found.)

Name and shame

Frustrated by managers circumnavigating the purchasing department when placing orders, this business runs a monthly list of invoices that have been paid for which there were no purchase orders raised. The list is then circulated to 'name and shame' offenders.

In practice

- Work with the buying department to get the very best value for money you can from your budget!

CAN I SPEAK TO...?

SOME SUPERMARKET PRICING just doesn't make sense.

Signs advertising special offers where instead of paying 99p each you can have two for £2 make you wonder what else doesn't stack up.

The more complex the pricing structure – or the more variety of discounts you offer different customers – the more likely you are to make mistakes.

And mistakes cost money. Some stores offer to refund you twice the difference should they price an item incorrectly – so they've got plenty to lose if they get it wrong.

The idea

Pricing matters. Every £1 you inadvertently give away on sales comes straight off your profit.

It might not surprise you to learn that few customers complain if undercharged and some even indulge in sharp practice by accessing prices from a cheaper price list.

Differential pricing

Aerospace companies often have two price lists – one for OE (Original Equipment) and another for spares with the latter having the higher prices. Unscrupulous customers may continue to order 'OE' when the components are actually to be sold on again as spares, allowing the customer to further enhance his margins. In this type of situation it's worth keeping an eagle eye on quantities ordered. This aerospace business, suspicious that this might be the case, now tracks equipment sales closely and makes sure they earn the appropriate margins.

Pricing lotteries

A customer's ability to access cheaper prices may be down to your own mis-management. Your pricing structure should be clear and consistently applied no matter who takes the order.

This business sold its products through a team of tele-sales operators who would quote prices to customers and enter the priced orders into the system. Updated price-lists were produced periodically, photocopied and handed out to operators. Not all operators. Operators who were there, who were not so busy on the phone that they were unaware that a new list had been issued, and who were not so distracted that they mislaid the sheet of paper and failed to update their records. It wasn't surprising that customers began to notice that the prices they were quoted depended on which operator they spoke to... and they soon learned who to ask for.

In practice

- Make sure there are clear controls on price-lists ensuring they are consistent throughout the organisation.

- Challenge any overly-complicated pricing structures – complexity breeds confusion that causes cost (see IDEA 22).

15 CAPITALISING ON YOUR INVESTMENT

When you invest in new facilities or processes (Fixed Assets) it is referred to as Capital Expenditure. You may well find that there is an onerous process you have to go through in order to be allowed to make these purchases.

At first sight it seems a little odd that such attention is given to Capital Expenditure decisions, as most businesses spend far more money each year on other things such as materials, consumables, overtime, utilities (Revenue Expenditure)... and it might appear that virtually everyone in the organisation is allowed to authorise those.

Why pick on Capital Expenditure for special treatment?

The idea

Because investing in facilities and processes is a strategic decision. When you choose your facilities and processes, you define your offering to the market. Your choice of land and buildings determines your geographic location. The selection of equipment determines the way you intend to pull materials through your business and turn them into final products. The vehicles you choose will shape your distribution capabilities.

You need to align your business to meet market needs (see IDEAS 81 & 94).

Who do you want to pay for the facilities and processes you have chosen? The customer.

Getting it right

The market will pay a price that rewards suppliers for meeting their needs. If a supplier chooses to do this inefficiently, the business will pay the cost – not the customer. Customers do not pay a premium to companies who choose to make things inappropriately.

If you make the wrong choices (and your competitors get it right), you will operate at a competitive disadvantage that could put you out of business.

Therefore the reason you may be required to jump through so many hoops before committing to this type of expenditure is because the company wants to maximise the probability of making the right decision.

Financial matters

When it comes to the financials, the investment appraisal is relatively simple – if you go ahead with the project, will the company be better off? Will the benefits outweigh the costs?

Or to be more precise, will the incremental cash inflows outweigh the incremental cash outflows?

Or to be more prosaic, will the savings you make more than outweigh the cost of the purchase.

So what kinds of cost improvements might be on offer?

Savings may include...

- reductions to manpower requirements;
- reduced scrap rates;
- lower maintenance charges;
- increased capacity with less machine down-time;

- reduced stock holding as a result of steadier throughput;

- lower energy bills

And of course the investment may have a positive effect on your sales.

You may be able to sell more without proportionately increasing your costs and therefore add to your profits; or you may be able to supply a higher quality product and increase your prices – and that impact goes straight to the bottom line!

In practice

- Make sure you have a process in place for authorising Capital Expenditure that is appropriate to the significance of purchasing decisions – and that you always use your specialists to negotiate the best deal (see IDEA 13)!

- Test each proposal by asking the question "Will the customer pay a price that rewards me for meeting his needs this way?". If he won't pay – you will.

CHEAPER BY DEFAULT

EVERYTIME ANYONE IN your business uses a resource you incur a cost. So you need to find ways to influence the choices they make.

The idea

Don't just tell people what things cost (see IDEA 71), also encourage them to make cost-effective choices by default.

Photocopying

Setting printer and photocopier defaults to black and white duplex copies can make savings on paper and cartridge costs (see IDEA 56).

This college encourages cost-effective photocopying choices not exactly by default, but by charging all printing costs against departmental budgets... except for printing done on the lowest cost-per-copy centralised machine.

Travel

Travel arrangements should default to your preferred hotel partner, or airline or travel agent with whom you've negotiated a corporate rate, or discounts, or retrospective rebates.

Standardisation

Encouraging designers to use standardised parts reduces the cost of holding stock, gives buyers the opportunity to negotiate better discounts, and helps mitigate some of the costly risks associated with new product introduction (see IDEAS 46 & 97).

Timing

Scheduling power-intensive activities (e.g. charging up fork-lift trucks) whenever you can to lowest tariff periods will save on your electricity bills (see IDEA 48).

Requisitions
This manufacturer used to have stores requisition forms that were blank so people would withdraw items from stores, often unaware that there were cheaper alternatives available that were just as fit for purpose. Not only were some choices ill-informed, inaccuracies in completing information (such as the account codes) resulted in difficulties in understanding and managing the spend (see IDEA 19).

Pre-printed requisition forms listing the preferred choice for the most commonly requested items (together with their account codes) have now replaced the blank forms. Should other items be required, the process requires the authorisation of a more senior manager. This improvement has made the better-value items the default choice and also enhanced the accuracy of management information.

The next improvement? Add the cost of items to the pre-printed list to discourage waste (see IDEA 71).

In practice

- Look for opportunities to direct the selection of purchases or timing of activities to the most cost-effective choice.

- However, do be careful that in trying to make improvements in for example, purchasing costs, you don't inadvertently end up costing the business more (see IDEA 49)!

CHECK-OUT ASSISTANTS ARE SUPPOSED TO CHECK

You've spent all that money setting up the store and filling it with stock. The store is busy with customers interested in what you have to offer and ready to pay you back for all your hard work.

But are your tills ringing? Should they be ringing more often than they are? You are at the mercy of your check-out or sales assistants.

The idea

Don't underestimate the importance of the calibre of your check-out or sales assistants.

We've all experienced those occasions when sales assistants are far more interested in discussing their social lives than taking our money – despite the fact that the money will be used to pay their salaries. The business doesn't just lose this sale but suffers manifold, as not only do we not return next time we need to shop, we also talk to our friends about the poor service.

If there are long queues at the check-out, potential customers tend to go elsewhere.

You do begin to suspect that in some stores there is an unofficial competition going on between assistants to see who can serve the fewest customers.

Discount store
Queues at the check-out in this discount clothing retail outlet build

as assistants seem more interested in developing their origami skills than by keeping lines moving. They fold items meticulously only to then bundle them together and shove them into an undersized carrier bag.

What was surprising were the tales of check-out staff repeatedly failing to check everything customers had brought to them and were willing to pay for. Staff at the tills of these businesses appear to have problems with their eyesight.

Café

This otherwise upright and virtuous acquaintance recounted how he had visited a café belonging to a well-known chain to buy a cup of tea and a scone. Reflecting on the occasion some time later he realised he had not been charged for the jam he had also put on his tray. Perhaps a minor slip. But as a manager himself he was interested in whether this was just a one-off event or whether there was a general lack of care in the checking process. It has now become a challenge to see on how many occasions he can visit the same café for his favoured snack without ever being charged for the pot of jam. He's still counting.

Garden centre

Another colleague explained the reason she preferred to shop at a certain garden centre. Fed up with constantly pointing out when they failed to charge her for all the items in her trolley...

In practice

- Make the recruitment, training and supervision of your sales team a priority.

  If you can't turn all your hard work back into cash again, you're not in business!

18 CHOOSE YOUR PARTNERS

WHAT'S THE DIFFERENCE between an employee and a supplier?

Very little other than that you pay one through the payroll and the other via an invoice. Just as you need to make sure you have the best team with the necessary skills working for you, you also need great suppliers. You are only as good as the weakest link in the chain.

So what makes a good supplier?

The idea

When you choose who you're going to work with, remember that it's not just a question of great prices – although that of course helps.

If you measure your purchasing performance on price savings alone you are in danger of ending up making some costly savings (see IDEA 49)!

For starters, you need suppliers who consistently deliver what you want, when you want it, to the specification you require, at a competitive price and who can offer you appropriate credit terms.

(That should take care of minimising the amount of money you have locked up in Working Capital... as long as you really do know what you want, when you want it, and the specification you need!)

But that's not enough.

Long-term relationships
Given the time and energy (and hence cost) you incur in finding new suppliers, you also need suppliers who are sustainable and

won't go to the wall leaving you empty-handed scurrying around for alternatives. (As soon as you see the word 'scurry' you may as well insert the word 'cost' as inevitably you throw £50 notes at the situation trying to get yourself out of a hole – see IDEA 22.)

And on top of all that, you need suppliers who want to do business with you.

You may question the rationale behind that statement. Surely the fact that they have taken your order means they want to be your supplier? Not necessarily.

Keep them on-side
In times of surplus capacity your supplier might be willing to take any business – even yours. But what happens when circumstances change and the balance of power shifts to the supplier? If you've played 'screw the supplier', messing them around making impossible demands and then not paying them in line with the agreed terms, you're asking for trouble.

That's exactly what this large manufacturing machining company did to its sub-contractors. These small, often family-run concerns, had spent years under the harsh rule of their customer, subjected to the whims of their master as a result of his poor scheduling and his reluctance to hand over money at the appropriate time. Having seen a number of their sister companies thoughtlessly thrown to the wolves whenever it suited their master, loyalty was in short supply.

Then came the business upturn. The master suddenly had a brimming order book and, unable to find sufficient additional capacity in-house, started placing substantial business with the sub-contractors. However, the sub-contractors, who were also inundated with work, could now start being selective about who they did business with...

Work together

You should see your suppliers as partners – if you get it right they should be as enthusiastic as you are at finding ways of working together to eliminate waste from both businesses.

This organisation bravely held a forum for its suppliers at which suppliers were invited to list problems they had (and therefore costs they were incurring) with their host in his position as customer. Scheduling (or lack of it) was the key complaint. Inevitably, the timeliness of payments also came up, as did other aspects such as packaging and transportation. But most intriguing was that when one supplier commented that he had problems with part numbers, another shrugged his shoulders and said he had been correcting the part numbers quoted on the customer's orders for the last 5 years as he knew what they really wanted to order... and he was right! Time for a proper fix (see IDEA 27).

Talk to your suppliers about what you buy. The supplier's salesman in IDEA 43 found a great way to win extra business while saving his customer's money by moving from selling parts to selling kits.

As partners, suppliers have a vested interest in your success at winning new orders – and keeping existing business. A buyer spoke of how highly he valued the relationship with a particular supplier who not only gave him great service – but who was also an excellent supporting act when asked to get directly involved with customers as and when the need arose.

Involving suppliers at the design stage can also pay great dividends as they can bring their expertise to the table, helping you find the most cost-effective way of meeting your customer's needs (see IDEA 97).

In practice

- Review the tenor of your relationships with suppliers – is it confrontational or is it co-operative?

- Remember that you are your supplier's customer – perhaps you should reflect on some of the criticisms you have of your customers?

- Ask suppliers to submit a consolidated invoice on a monthly basis rather than multiple individual invoices throughout the month, as this can reduce the cost of processing and paying invoices – and can effectively extend your credit terms.

CODED MESSAGES

How do you know whether you're improving if you don't measure? You have to measure to manage.

If you're going to manage your costs, you therefore have to measure them – which means making sure you understand exactly what you're spending and what you're spending it on.

Accounts codes. Timesheets and shopfloor bookings.

Possibly not the most exciting topics.

But if you don't know what you're spending your money on and have the information available to enable you to have a reasonable understanding of what your products cost to make, how are you going to direct and measure the effectiveness of those improvement activities?

The idea

Coding matters. When expenditure or usage is authorised, the signer should also be agreeing to the cost being charged to the specific category of cost for which they have a budget. Not only should you be unable to 'dump' costs against somebody else's budget, neither should you play 'trade-offs' within your own budget responsibilities by deliberately mis-coding expenditure to categories where you have a 'bit of headroom'.

If you have been able to make savings on one type of expenditure, that does not authorise you to spend it elsewhere! Remember that what matters is not the size of your budget, but how effectively you use the money you spend (see IDEA 69). Somebody else in the organisation may have much greater need for those released resources than you have. Pooling savings and then re-directing the resources will help your business get best value from every £1 available (see IDEA 35).

Deciphering information

How many account codes should you have? It's a question of getting the balance right. Too many codes and costs become so fragmented that it can be difficult to see the big picture and the choice of coding somewhat judgemental. Too few and managing the costs become difficult without wasting time continually analysing what has gone into the bucket.

And while on the subject of buckets, it's worth mentioning cupboards.

While there should be strict controls on accounts codes, the ease with which new codes could be generated ironically proved a blessing in this organisation as it highlighted an ever-growing category of stock that this new production manager couldn't reconcile to any location of which he was aware. He finally tracked it down – a cupboard into which rejected parts had been tucked away waiting further action. Or eventually, the purchase of a bigger cupboard (see IDEA 84).

Exceptionals

It's also very helpful to log exceptional spends. When reviewing how you're doing and looking ahead in planning resources for the future, it's a great idea to be able to differentiate between underlying costs and 'one-offs'. Purchasing departments often do this for materials by identifying orders to be included in the database for future estimating purposes, and those to be set aside because the price agreed was either exceptionally high (perhaps a 'panic' order allowing the supplier to recover the costs of laying on an additional overtime shift) or exceptionally low (possibly down to buying a much larger volume than usual). It might be informative to track how often 'exceptional' orders are placed as an indication of how well-controlled the organisation is!

In practice

- Review your coding systems – are the codes relevant and at an appropriate level of detail?

- Audit the accuracy of coding – if it's not correct, you're busy wasting time and money collecting misinformation.

- Look at your part numbering systems as well. You can't rely on your suppliers (and everyone else) to be mind-readers (see IDEA 18).

20 COMPLEXITY BREEDS COST

Do you offer a wide-range of products or services? ... to many different customers? ... in many different markets? ... do you have lots of different suppliers?

While some diversification may be appropriate to reduce risk, too much can sink the business.

The idea

The complexity of your business will play a key factor in determining how much it costs to run. For example, many businesses claim to make great margins on their spares, but may overlook the additional costs they incur through complexity (see IDEAS 61 & 64).

Consider the small local village shop and its inability to negotiate massive discounts from suppliers. To be sustainable there must be a sufficient number of customers prepared to pay a significant convenience premium on enough goods for the owners to make a living. For customers to come through the door, the shop must offer an adequate range of goods to meet their needs. But every time that range is increased so do the costs (e.g. extra money is tied up, extra space is required, there is increased risk of obsolescence either because of sell-by dates or fashion), and hence the convenience premium required to keep the store open increases and...

A delicate balance.

Don't try to be all things to all people – unless they'll pay you for the privilege.

Premium business

For most businesses it is a great idea to reduce inventory to release cash to either reduce debt (and hence interest costs), or to use profitably elsewhere in the business (see IDEA 40). But not always. This business supplies a range of components used for repairing oil-drilling equipment in the North Sea. When a rig is down, the customer sends a helicopter to collect the required part.

The cost of the part is virtually irrelevant.

What matters is availability.

If the customer rings and they don't have the part in stock he will call the next person on his list... and may well not call this business first next time. The key success criterion here is product availability with the customer prepared to pay a price that rewards the supplier handsomely for the level of investment and degree of complexity.

In practice

- Reflect on the range of products or services you offer and the diversity of your customer base.

- Review the profitability not just of each product or service you offer but also the categories of customers you serve.

- Look at the advantages of standardisation discussed in IDEA 46 and consider the virtues of simplicity.

21 CUPCAKES, CHAMPAGNE AND MURDER

THIS IS NOT a book about great advertising ideas – but it is a book about getting the most you can out of everything you spend. And that includes advertising.

The idea

While the impact of any particular advertising spend may be difficult to gauge without expensive market research, here are some ideas that have worked for other people.

Something extra

If you already have a customer there in front of you, make sure you take the opportunity to meet as many of their needs as possible. Train staff to advertise bolt-on products.

In a restaurant you have a maximum number of covers from which to make a living. Make sure your customers are asked if they would like those added extras that bring in additional income and that their glasses are not left empty. Well-trained personable staff can make a great deal of difference to your bottom line (see IDEA 77)!

Market ploys

This enterprising young lady makes and sells delicious cupcakes. When at events such as farmers' markets, she takes her laptop and 'twitters' where she is and what's going on. Customers approach her stand saying they'd just picked up that she was there – so she knows this works. Of course once they've tasted her cakes then she's got them hooked anyway!

A bar-gain

This nightclub advertises a special deal. Parties of 6 people or more are given a voucher on entry for a bottle of champagne for £6. Making the move from bars to the clubs, people will try to make sure they bring 5 friends with them to be entitled to this bargain. Of course once the extra people are there, they will drink more than just a glass of champagne, the more people there are in the club the more business it attracts anyway... and by the way, the bottle of champagne costs the club owner £2.

Recommendations

Let your customers do the advertising for you! Ask happy customers if they'd be willing to be a reference, display your advertising material or pass your business card on to others. By asking new customers how they heard of you, you can trace the recommendation. Don't forget to express thanks appropriately – often a brief note or call is quite enough. (Some businesses brochures will ask you to recommend another contact for them in return for a free entry into a draw or for a discount on your purchase. While the vendor hopes to thereby target his advertising in a more focused way, you should beware friendships with those who take up these offers.)

Networking Groups

These can offer a win-win in connecting people and forming links in supply chains (see IDEA 33).

Get the picture

The entrepreneur who runs these murder-mystery dinners and other entertainment events has found a way to massacre his advertising costs by using edited digital photographs for his promotional literature. Once he's finalised the details, he mails his order for 'reprints' to the local supermarket cutting out the printer altogether. For the volumes he requires, this results in a substantial saving in advertising costs – and a great-looking high quality flyer!

In practice

- Every £1 spent on advertising comes straight off the bottom line – so make sure you earn a return on your investment.

- Avoid setting your advertising budget as a % sales – logically it should be the other way round! And as there is a tendency to spend whatever is in the budget, it's usually much better to start with the advertising activities you're planning to carry out, and then link them directly to the budget you're going to set for sales. This will focus on the intention of the spend... to bring in that business!

22. DO YOU HAVE A HOCKEY-STICK?

You've worked hard and done well. Those materials have been turned into quality products and the customer is ready to receive them. How well are you going to manage those last few critical steps of getting the product to the customer and him paying you for all your efforts?

The idea

Take a look at the workload in your despatch department. When you walk in at the beginning of the month do you find very little activity... but as time goes on, things start to pick up gradually until the last few days of the month when there's complete chaos and limitless overtime?

That's the hockey-stick.

Some goods won't get despatched – or even if they do, they won't get invoiced on time and that's going to cost the business money (see IDEA 85). Those goods that do go out are done in a rush and you know what happens then.

Mistakes.

In satisfying the customer, you're looking to be reimbursed for all that hard work that's been going on.

Does the customer pay if you ship the wrong goods? Or if the goods are incorrectly packaged and arrive damaged? Or if required accompanying documentation is omitted?

... or if the goods go to the wrong destination?

Just checking

An important order for a very large, heavy and expensive item was scheduled for completion by the end of this company's financial year. As the clock kept ticking, more and more cost was thrown at the project as increasing numbers of people got involved in 'managing' the product through the process (a classic example of manufacturing 'shove' rather than customer 'pull'). To everyone's great relief the product was eventually finished, loaded on to the back of a lorry and shipped off to the airport from where, at tremendous cost to the business, it would be air-freighted to the eagerly waiting customer. It was only some time later, amidst the self-congratulatory celebrations, that the salesman tapped the despatch manager on the shoulder and said, "You did pick up on the fact that it's to go to Sydney, Canada, didn't you?"

Of course by this time it was on its way to Australia...

And it doesn't just happen in despatch.

Wherever there is unplanned or rushed activity, there are likely to be mistakes.

And mistakes end up costing you money to put right.

In practice

- Look for the pressure-points in your own business.

- Identify ways that processes and procedures can be re-engineered so that work can be sensibly and evenly paced to maximise the probability of getting it 'right first time'.

23 **DOES ANYONE USE THIS?**

IF YOU DO something, it requires time and possibly materials and therefore costs money.

While attention may be paid to the margins made on business done with outside customers, what about your internal ones?

Who do you supply with products or services or information?

What 'value' do they place on these?

Is it worth doing?

The idea

Look critically at how you meet the needs of your internal customers.

A lecturer from a leading university told me how he'd called into the departmental administration office a couple of weeks before the start of the new academic year. Chaos, pandemonium and the onset of multiple breakdowns lay before him. When sensitively enquiring as to the reason behind this, he was told that every year all new students had to be provided with a CD loaded with information from the relevant university websites. This took the staff two weeks of intensive activity.

Why were they doing this?

By the time they had produced the CDs, the information on the websites would have changed... and their customers, the students, were far more adept than they were with IT and would tend to go straight to the website in the first place. Why not just signpost the sites as part of the welcome mail sent to all students?

Now seen as a visionary saviour by staff who were told that this activity was no longer required, the lecturer couldn't wait to tell them his latest idea about rationalising the plethora of consent forms students had to sign on their arrival... (see IDEA 87)

In practice

- Identify the 'outputs' (products, services and information) you supply to your internal customers.

- 'Walk' your outputs to your customer to ensure you are giving them the service they require, i.e.:

  - what they want

  - in the form they want it

  - in the timescale they need it

  - with the frequency required

  If nobody needs it – don't do it!

24 DOES EVERYONE KNOW WHAT CAUSED THE FIRE?

MISTAKES HAPPEN. BUT the same mistake shouldn't happen twice.

The great advantage of working in an organisation is that you shouldn't have to learn from just your own mistakes!

The idea

While it's important to establish the root cause of a problem (see IDEA 27), it's also important to communicate what's happened if you're going to prevent people (even different people) repeating the same mistake.

You need a business culture where problems are openly discussed and resolved and where the focus is on causes rather than culprits.

If you don't communicate causes, people will carry on in blissful ignorance.

Buyers will continue to make purchase price savings, unaware that the costs outweigh the benefits (see IDEA 49).

Designers will continue to build in features that are either unwanted (see IDEA 43) or to design products in a way that cannot be made in a cost-effective manner (see IDEA 97).

And feedback needs to be timely...

Close the loop
This contract engineering company would bid for contracts equipped

with estimated costs prepared by the specialist estimating department who reported to the sales side of the business. Some months later the sales team would hear whether their bid was successful and, if so, build into their reports the margin they expected to make. The contract would then be handed over to manufacturing and attention would turn to the next bit of potential new business.

These were fairly long-term contracts and month-by-month the cost accounting department, located at some distance from the estimating department, would gradually collect the actual costs incurred. Only at the end of the contract, when the actual margin earned was reported, would there be any dialogue between the two departments – almost inevitably a heated debate about why the estimated and actual margins were so very different. Not only was there a great deal of wasted time and effort expended in often unsuccessful attempts to try and reconcile the two figures, but with no feedback loop of actual cost information back into the estimating system, there was also little likelihood of the problem ever being resolved.

Following reorganisation, team members are now responsible not just for estimating but also for collecting, analysing and reporting actual costs against those estimates. Management have an early warning of cost drift and the quality of estimates is improved.

Forum
If your business is part of a group, it can be helpful to have opportunities to share experiences – in a timely manner. It was so disappointing to overhear a discussion between manufacturing managers working for the same group where one was bemoaning a regretted purchase of a certain brand of equipment only to have a sympathetic response from the other along the lines of "Yes, I know. We bought one of those a year or so back and have never been able to get it working properly..."

In practice

Make sure that when you dig down to establish the root cause of a problem, you don't just leave it there to seed but pull it out, show everyone what damage it was causing and then get rid of it. Or, to put it another way, don't just put out the fire (see IDEA 27) – take away the matches.

DOES SIZE MATTER?

Do you throw away tools because they have lost their size (e.g. drills)?

Have you checked whether these tools could be used in other areas where tolerances are not so critical?

Do you program in the use of expensive specialist cutting-tools (e.g. multi-dimensional reamers) instead of standard tools for straight-forward tasks such as circular interpolation when there is a cheaper one in the tool holder?

The idea

Challenge specifications to make sure you're not wasting your money on unwarranted 'quality'. This principle should be applied throughout your business... to materials, packaging... even documentation (see IDEA 2).

Standardising where possible might get you out of a jam.

Critical differences

This components manufacturer makes a range of products for a particular customer. One part in particular is difficult to make with very tight tolerances on a critical aspect of the design and there had always been a substantial scrap rate on orders for these parts. If it had been possible, the design would have been changed but commercially this was impossible. Therefore (while having strong words with the design department to ensure that the challenging aspects of this design were not replicated in future product lines – see IDEA 24), it was a question of making the most of a difficult job.

While the business supplies this customer with a wide-range of final components, there is commonality in the initial stages of the process. Some of these components require more critical tolerances than others. Rather than launch orders destined for specific part numbers, the business now initiates manufacture of the generic stage of the design.

At the final point of commonality, the part-built components are tested and sorted with those meeting the highest specification going on to fill orders for the most difficult parts. Others can be used for those products with the less stringent tolerances.

In practice

◉ Look for instances of 'over-specification' in your business.

- Do you always need the highest quality tools, equipment and materials for everything you do?

- Are you doing things 'better' than the customer wants and is prepared to pay for?

◉ Take a look at IDEA 46 for other ideas of how standardisation can help you control costs and save money.

And remember that size doesn't necessarily determine cost (see IDEA 72)!

26 DON'T BELIEVE EVERYTHING YOU READ!

Is IT IMPORTANT to know how much your products or services cost?

It is if you want to understand your business and know where you're making profits (or losses).

If you don't...

- How do you work out whether it's a great idea to find ways to sell more?

- How do you judge the impact of a change in your sales mix?

- While cost doesn't usually determine price (see IDEA 94) you still need to know when to walk away from the negotiating table.

- How do you focus cost improvement activities – and know if they've worked?

You make all sorts of decisions based on your understanding of cost – but can you believe what you are told? Is the information you are given appropriate for the decision you are taking?

The idea

Understand the basis of the costing information you're given, and therefore whether it is fit for the purpose for which you intend to use it.

Many companies used a method of costing products known as absorption costing. This method takes business costs (other than direct materials and sometimes direct labour) and charges them out to products on the back of the labour hours or machine hours each product or service requires. The rate at which they are charged out is often referred to as a cost rate or burden rate.

Take a look at what goes into this rate in your business.

Whose payroll costs?
- You'll probably find it includes the cost of employing most people from the person who sweeps the shopfloor through clerical staff, supervisors and managers right through to the managing director.

Which expenses?
- Possibly everything other than direct materials – so that means rent, rates, utilities, consumables, packaging, transport, stationery, travel, advertising...

That's not fair!
Does every hour of work carried out on a product or service really cost your business the same amount of money?

You love it when you see certain products on this week's production schedule. Having been well-designed and with a great supply chain, they run through your process like a dream requiring very little support. Assume you have a cost rate of £80 per hour for every hour a product takes to make. If this product requires an hour of work it will pick up £80 of business cost.

But what about the product line everyone dreads making? It is poorly designed and suppliers have difficulty delivering materials that meet the required specification. When you eventually receive materials that pass inspection, they are brought to the shopfloor where a team of people stand round the machine trying to 'nurse' it through the process. It also takes an hour to make and therefore picks up the same amount (£80) of business costs.

There will always be 'winners and losers' with any costing method, but you need to make sure that the information you get out of the system doesn't skew reality to such an extent that you start making wrong decisions.

Think about the demand life-cycle of a product or service (see IDEA 64).

Stars shine brighter
On product launch, demand grows rapidly (the 'star' stage). During this period, products require a great deal of support as you sort out initial problems with supply chains and your own processes. Products therefore tend to be under-costed.

Does it matter?

Yes, because if you understood just how much it was costing the business to get through this stage you might take a fresh look at a number of issues including:

- How much money should you spend at the development stage getting things right before you start?

- How many products can you afford to have at the 'star' stage at any one time?

When the product is running steadily through the business (the 'cow' stage) it requires relatively little support therefore tends to get over-costed.

So what?

Cows to the slaughter
If businesses overestimate the cost of making these products they risk killing off their life-support machines – their cash-generating cows (see IDEA 52)!

When markets become more competitive and prices start to fall, businesses drop these highly profitable product lines in the belief they are loss-making. Products that the company are excellent at making get sub-contracted out or outsourced to 'low-cost economies' (see IDEA 89).

Dogged by complexity
Many businesses will tell you that they make massive margins on their spares. They may make good margins – but probably not as good as they think. As the product reaches the final stage of its demand cycle and volumes start to fall away (the 'dog' stage) the tendency is to under-cost products. Managing 'dogs' increases complexity and complexity causes cost. The potential additional cost of smaller production runs and hence more frequent change-overs can be tackled by re-evaluating the appropriate process for this change in pattern of demand (see IDEA 47), but there is a tendency to overlook issues such as the hidden costs of selling 'one-off' parts when suppliers have minimum order quantities (see IDEA 61).

In practice

- Take a look at your costing system and understand its strengths and weaknesses – is it appropriate for decision-making?

- Make sure designers get to know which are those 'loved' and 'hated' products – if your products are designed in a way that results in them being difficult to make, you will be incurring extra costs the designer will probably have overlooked and will not be evident from most costing systems.

- Engage your cost czar (see IDEA 92) in discussions of how to present information in a meaningful way – thereby avoiding inadvertently taking a one-way trip down the death-spiral (see IDEA 73)!

27

DON'T JUST PUT OUT THE FIRE

IN YOUR BUSINESS things can go wrong.

So you (along with everyone else) have not yet achieved perfection.

Every time things don't go perfectly – e.g. you scrap some products; fail to deliver to your customers on time; or have your goods returned as faulty – it costs the company money (see IDEA 90).

We all make mistakes.

Businesses, however, can't afford to keep repeating the same mistakes so you need to find out not just what went wrong, but also why it went wrong.

The idea

Keep digging until you find the root cause of your problems.

There is a saying that if you ask 'Why?' five times you will find the real reason behind what is happening.

The real problem might not lie where you think it does...

There's no smoke...
Take the case of the fainting night-shift worker. Let's call him Joe. Starting his shift alongside his fellow-workers Joe would always seem fine and all would be well until, on a regular basis, after returning from his break, he would start to complain of feeling unwell.

His supervisor eventually became suspicious that this was all too convenient and one night insisted he carried on working. Joe fainted. Unable to identify what was going on Joe was transferred to the day-shift. The same thing happened. Everybody else doing the same work continued to be fine. Was Joe putting it on? By now improbable. Was he allergic to something he was eating or drinking on his break? Unlikely. Was it something to do with the fact that he needed reminding to put on the protective gloves provided? But the supervisor had had to remind others of this too and they didn't have this problem. Only by shadowing Joe did the supervisor work out what was causing the problem.

Joe did not wash his hands when he went for his break. But neither did a couple of the others. What made the difference was that Joe was the only one who didn't wash his hands but then proceeded to roll his own cigarette. When he lit it, the residue of one of the chemical sprays he used for his work, (which he had now transferred to the paper), would vaporise, creating a gas similar to phosgene – the chemical weapon known during WWI as 'nerve gas'. No wonder he felt faint!

When things go wrong, you need to get right down to the root cause of the problem – and fix it (see IDEA 24). In this case it was relatively easy. All Joe had to do was remember to use his gloves and wash his hands – and even better, also give up smoking!

In practice

- Think about how open people in your business are when it comes to dealing with mistakes. If there is a 'blame culture' where problems are either swept under the carpet or into another area, it makes it difficult to untangle those roots.

- Take a look at techniques such as the 5 whys and Cause and Effect Analysis (also known as fishbone or *Ishikawa* diagrams) that can be used to nail* the real reason for the problem.

- Make sure that whenever you find the cause you also implement the fix (see IDEA 24).

- Get yourself a rottweiler (See IDEA 51)!

* Remember the proverb?

> *For want of a nail the shoe was lost;*
>
> *For want of a shoe the horse was lost;*
>
> *For want of a horse the man was lost;*
>
> *For want of a man the battle was lost;*
>
> *For want of a battle the kingdom was lost;*
>
> *And all for the want of a nail.*

Perhaps the earliest example of using the 5 whys?

28

DON'T STOP BEFORE YOU'VE ARRIVED AT YOUR DESTINATION!

THERE'S ONLY ONE step of the Working Capital cycle (see IDEA 40) that brings any financial benefit to the business – the customer paying you.

And yet all too often celebrations are premature. Making the product (production targets) or moving your money into your customer's warehouse (sales targets) are merely staging posts.

None of this is worth doing unless the customer pays you for what you've done. You haven't completed your journey around the cycle until the customer has handed over the money. If you stop short of this you may as well have just sat in a corner of the office shredding those £50 notes again (see IDEA 90).

What can you do to make sure you get paid on time?

The idea

Some customers have to decide, at the end of every month, which of their suppliers are to be paid. Make sure you're at the top of the list by being professional in the way you manage those debts.

This sole trader has found from experience that her customers respond better to invoice-chasing if they believe there is a specialist on the case. So she has invented another persona for this purpose.

Invoice promptly and in line with your customer's processing requirements. Get to know your customers – not just the people who place orders with you but also those who receive deliveries, sign-off for quality, process invoices and authorise payments.

Don't wait to chase up late payments. 'Nurse' your invoices through your customer's payment process by courteously ensuring each step has taken place smoothly, leaving no excuses for non-payment. If there are problems sort them out before they result in arrears. Good debtor management can look remarkably like excellent supplier service!

In practice

- Build customer records with the names and contact details of the key players at each stage of the payment process.

- Remember that if your customer hasn't been invoiced he probably isn't going to pay... (see IDEA 32)

- Manage your debts to avoid overdues – but if you're still having problems take a look at IDEA 95 and get to the root cause of why your customers aren't paying.

29 DON'T TRY TO DO EVERYTHING!

GONE ARE THE days of 'big is beautiful' when businesses raced to acquire competitors, suppliers and customers alike. In the face of fierce competitive pressures, companies are targeting their energies (and their resources) on what they do best.

The idea

Focus on your core competencies – those activities on which you can earn a sustainable living – and think creatively about realigning your product or service portfolio to improve profitability.

A lesson for us all

Unable to continue to justify its own training department, this insurance company supported their training managers in setting up their own training business by providing them with subsidised facilities and a guaranteed order book, in return for a supply commitment on the provision of specialist courses.

Suit yourself

No, not a gentleman's outfitter but an over-grown subsidiary of an international business that had, over the years, developed new product lines that had little, if any, synergy with their core product. Once transplanted to appropriate habitats, where processes could be tailored to products, the cuttings thrived and the garden flourished.

Charitable thoughts

Unable to run much-needed family support activities throughout their region on its own, this charity encourages groups of volunteers to come forward and run their own sessions by offering free expertise, administration – and step-by-step help with the otherwise overwhelming maze of compliance documentation!

Corporate partnerships

By organising a corporate partnership, it is possible to use your competitor's resources – such as transport networks, physical structures, raw materials, knowledge, and customer reputation – to realise the full potential of an ambitious idea that would otherwise rely on your acquiring an unfeasibly large number of new resources. Such deals can be negotiated either by giving partners a share of profits, or by arranging a mutual relationship where they are allowed to use your resources in return.

Oneworld Alliance – a partnership between ten major airlines (British Airways, Cathay Pacific, Finnair, Iberia, LAN, Qantas, Japan Airlines, Malév, Royal Jordanian, and American Airlines) – utilises corporate partnerships to offer a service they could not provide separately. The service is an inclusive, low-cost round-the-world fare where customers pay a one-off fee to travel to a wide range of global destinations. Because customers can travel on any airline within the Oneworld Alliance, the scheme offers the customer the opportunity to travel to over 600 destinations in 135 countries. This highly successful service provides a helpful method of complying with the restrictive rules in the aviation industry governing ownership of airlines, in a way that benefits customers.

In practice

- Be brutally honest with yourself about which aspects of your business you do well and make money out of.

- Understand the price you're paying if your heart rules your head.

- Look for fresh approaches to working with customers, suppliers and even competitors.

30 EXCESSIVE BEHAVIOUR

How DID YOU end up with all that surplus inventory?

Not only is surplus inventory tying up your money and costing you interest, but it could end up costing you even more.

While the inventory may well be of items that you're currently using or selling, if there are too many on the shelf you may eventually have to discount them heavily to shift them – or even write them off. And that's like putting money straight into the shredder.

The idea

Tackle the root cause of why the surplus inventory is there to stop it from building up again and divert existing excess holdings from their journey to the skip.

Could it be that...
Worried about unreliable suppliers or long lead times, you bought more than was needed at the time (see IDEA 18)?

Do designers re-invent the wheel every time with little regard to the benefits of standardisation – or even what you already have in inventory (see IDEAS 36 & 46)?

Do you measure your buyers' performance by their ability to make purchase price savings, thereby encouraging them to buy in bulk (see IDEA 10)?

Is the problem linked to the way you sell spares (see IDEA 61)?

Lifetime sentences
What if design changes mean components are no longer required?

What if fashions change and the 'must-have' items gather dust on the shelf? What if the item has a limited shelf-life?

In stores where items have limited shelf lives, it is important that regular housekeeping monitors usage and that items are displayed appropriately on the shelves. Try not to replenish shelves if there are items already out there that need shifting soon. Customers have a knack of reaching to the back of shelves to get products with later sell-by dates.

Make sure that your staff do not have an incentive to deliberately allow items to go out of date!

In this store, staff would 'forget' to bring older inventory to the front of the shelf. Why? Because when the shop closed at the end of each day, items that had then reached their expiry date were sold at 1p a time to staff.

Do you create 'shelf life' for items such as personalised stationery? How often does information on your headed notepaper change?

When companies have 'makeovers' (or are acquired by other organisations) they will need to revise their stationery. How much redundant inventory will there be left sitting on the shelf?

Who decides to change details on pre-printed forms and how do you manage existing inventory run-out?

In practice

- Be aware of everything in your business that has a limited life.

- Pay particular attention to how inventory of these items is managed... treat them as though they have a countdown timer attached to them, reminding you that time is running out!

FINDING GEMS

WHAT IS YOUR company's most valuable resource?

Your people.

They may not be valued on your Balance Sheet but they are the 'creativity' that allows you to take the things that are on the Balance Sheet (buildings, equipment, vehicles, inventory...) and use them to make products (or deliver services) that the market wants and is willing to pay for.

The idea

To make a sustainable living from the business, you need to have both the right things on your Balance Sheet and the right people creating value.

Your choice of people can make or break the business.

If you don't already have people with the right skill-sets you need to train existing staff or recruit.

This isn't a book about recruitment strategies. But when you recruit you are making an investment in people.

When investing in new equipment, you are usually faced with forging your way through a protracted process to consider all possible options and then justifying your choice (see IDEA 15).

Your choice of people can be even more critical to business survival.

Finding talent

Here are some ideas that have worked for other people:

- Ask around. Personal recommendations can identify suitable applicants who are not necessarily actively job-hunting.

- Check out local websites if applicable – those considering changing jobs may be accessing these rather than signing on at agencies.

- Be wary of incentives. While there may be some great financial incentives to take on people who have, for example, been out of work for a long time, this could be a false economy if they do not have, or are unable to acquire in a timely and cost-effective manner, the skills you are looking for.

- Statistics show that apprenticeships not only provide a good route to equipping employees with the specific skills required by your business but that they can also result in a high retention rate... and you can usually access government funding.

- Internships can offer you the opportunity to see potential employees at work in your business before making a long-term commitment.

- Build relationships with colleges and universities. Educational institutions are often very enthusiastic to be able to show evidence of their links to businesses and may be able to provide mentored students to carry out tasks for 'work experience' or more challenging problem-solving research work.

Close relationships with training providers can help you identify and access the best students and may prove useful in other ways...

Put to the test

Certification conditions meant that the products made by this business had to go through a specific type of testing (NDT) before being shipped. Only those with the relevant qualifications could carry out this procedure. Most activities required only the basic level of qualification but there was an occasional need for higher skills – and people with such skills proved to be like gold dust. Suitably qualified people with these higher skills were difficult to recruit, and investing in training up other people proved a waste of money as they invariably left shortly after gaining their qualifications for lucrative opportunities elsewhere. Fed up with being held to ransom by the in-house team, this manager found his solution elsewhere. At the local college. The tutor for the NDT qualification now supports the business with the higher skills required on an ad hoc basis – and proved invaluable when, in an emergency resulting from possible technical problems with a product, the manager had to rapidly build a team with NDT expertise to go to all corners of the world to check out products in situ.

Interviewing

When interviewing, try to assess whether the interviewee will work well with other people. Before hiring a maverick, make sure that the advantages will outweigh the costs (see IDEA 51)! Some organisations require recruits for senior positions not just to take personality profiling tests, but also to have a one-on-one with a psychologist to assess whether they will fit in well with the corporate culture.

And remember... what goes around can come around. Treat your interviewees fairly and courteously because, as this manager found out, at some not-too-far-distant future the roles may be reversed. When this happens it can pay to have kept those notes you made...

References

When it comes to references, consider contacting the referee over the phone as they will have less opportunity to prepare a carefully worded answer.

Probationary periods

Having made your choice and appointed your new team member make sure you use the probationary period properly to monitor and assess their work. Judge how they respond to constructive feedback. This is one of those rare opportunities where you get a chance for a 'trial marriage' before making a long-term commitment.

Make the most of it.

In practice

- While you're going to want value-for-money on your recruitment activities, make sure you access the best applicants.

- Go for quality, not quantity. Measure the effectiveness of your recruitment spend not on the volume of applications but the quality of the applicants.

- Ironically, the more applicants you have, the greater the risk of overlooking that gem...

GET IT INVOICED!

DOES YOUR BUSINESS have a get-it-out-the-door mentality?

Does everyone breathe a sigh of relief and head for the coffee-machine as the lorry disappears down the road on its way to the customer?

Haven't you forgotten something?

The idea

Not only do you want the customer to pay you for what you do – you also want him to pay for it as soon as possible. The longer you have to wait, the more capital you need to invest in the business just to keep it turning (see IDEA 40) and hence the more you're going to have to spend on interest payments.

To get the money in as fast as possible not only do you have to try to negotiate the shortest credit periods you can... you also have to raise an invoice!

You'd be surprised how often this gets overlooked or put aside to deal with later when there's a quiet moment to 'catch up with the paperwork'. If invoices are not raised promptly and accurately you're going to pay the price for it later when you come to try to collect that all-important cash. Even delaying a day can end up costing you money (see IDEA 85). But there can be other reasons than procrastination for delays in invoicing.

Changes in the market – Development costs
Many businesses have lived through an era when they could invoice the customer for development work before entering the production phase. However, most markets now require suppliers to spread the

recovery of these costs over an agreed initial quantity of production items. This means that the business has to finance the costs incurred for development over a longer time period, increasing their business investment and hence their interest costs. And of course if the customer then moves their schedules out to the right... (see IDEA 6).

Management focus – Milestone payments
Some longer-term contracts allow progress payments to be invoiced and paid upon reaching given milestones. While those involved in delivering the contract may well be avidly pouring over Gantt charts to map their progress, do they understand the commercial terms of the contract? Do they have their priorities right? A critical part of project-management is to understand where the trigger-points for invoicing are and put systems in place to make sure the trigger is pulled.

... and look out for those TBAs (see IDEA 70)!

In practice

- Focus on your destination – the customer paying you for all your hard work.

- Most customers will not pay without an invoice.

- Look at the various ways invoices should be being triggered by your business and ensure there are no obstacles in the way.

- Once you've invoiced make sure you collect the cash (see IDEA 28)!

33 GETTING HELP... AND HELPING OTHERS

Business may be competitive – but not everyone is competing against you!

The idea

Draw on others for expertise and to strengthen your negotiating position.

Neighbours

Trading estates are full of businesses incurring swathes of cost. There may be opportunities to use your collective purchasing power to negotiate better discounts or lower rates for services such as window-cleaning, gardening, catering and cleaning. Perhaps you could provide venues for each other for 'off-site' meetings?

Government agencies

Get value for money from your taxes by using government funded organisations that offer help and advice either to particular sectors or in specified geographic areas. A simple search on the internet will get you started and you can also ask around your contacts for where they've had good advice.

Expertise

Think about who might have the specific expertise you need... or will know a man who does. The factory inspector is usually regarded in a similar light to the tax inspector, but this one stopped a manager being exploited in his attempt to salvage his business following a fire (see IDEA 74).

Networking

Neighbourhood networking groups can also work well in helping develop mutually beneficial relationships, particularly for those in smaller businesses, or provide 'colleagues' and support for those working from home.

In IDEA 24 it was pointed out that one of the great advantages of working in an organisation is that you shouldn't have to learn from just your own mistakes. Cheltenham Connect Skillspace is a neighbourhood initiative providing networking opportunities for an eclectic group of business members who all have a story to tell – and experiences to share.

You may find some unlikely partners and colleagues (see IDEA 82)!

At a recent Skillspace meeting following a talk on the business opportunities offered by the latest social networking techniques, lessons could be traded not just with the homeworker from a multinational IT business and the builder who spends his evenings playing calypso gigs, but also with the young entrepreneur who had just started up a business making delicious cupcakes (see IDEA 21)!

In practice

- Look for opportunities to work with others to find those win-wins.

- Don't soldier on alone when there is plenty of help available – and often for free!

34 GO FORTH AND MULTIPLY

WHAT MATTERS IN a business is not profit, but profitability. If Tiny & Slick only makes a profit of £10,000 but Large & Sluggish makes a profit of £100,000 who has performed best? You can't tell unless you know how much they had to invest to earn that profit. If Tiny & Slick invested £40,000, they've done well earning a 25% return on their investment. If Large & Sluggish, on the other hand, had to invest £1,000,000 in their business, then they've only managed a paltry 10% return.

The idea

In seeking to improve your financial performance, you need to look for ways to either improve your profit or improve the effectiveness of your investment – or preferably, both!

As you have just seen, profitability is measured as :

$$\frac{\text{Profit}}{\text{Investment (Net Capital Employed)}} \quad X \quad 100 \ \%$$

(Net Capital Employed (NCE) is the amount invested in your business and is equivalent to the sum of money tied up in Fixed Assets and Working Capital).

If you want to improve your profitability, it's helpful to break the above calculation down into two constituent parts that, multiplied together, come back to the original formula.

Profit		Sales		Profit	
———— x 100%	=	————	x	———— x 100%
NCE		NCE		Sales

These parts are known as:		**Asset Turn**		**Profit margin**

Say you had a return of 20%. It could comprise:

	Asset Turn		**Profit margin**
	1	x	20%
or	2	x	10%
or	4	x	5%

... in fact, there are endless possibilities!

If you want to improve your return, you therefore need to improve your Asset Turn or improve your Profit margin or better still, improve both and get that multiplier effect!

Multiple attractions

	Asset Turn		**Profit margin**
Let's assume you currently have :	2	x	10%
If you improve your Asset Turn by 10% it becomes	2.2	x	10% = 22%
If instead you improve your Profit Margin by 10% it becomes	2	x	11% = 22%
But if you can improve both by 10%...	2.2	x	11% = 24.2%

Want to improve your Asset Turn?
You've got two options.

You can either increase your sales without proportionately increasing your investment, or you can maintain the level of sales while squeezing surplus investment out of the business.

Want to improve your margin?
Once again you've got two options.

You can either increase your sales without proportionately increasing your costs, or you can maintain the level of sales while eliminating unnecessary costs in the business.

In practice

- If you want to look at ways to improve your sales you could start with IDEA 66.

- If squeezing investment is your thing, then it's worth taking a look at IDEA 40 for starters.

- If it's unnecessary costs you're after then before you run amok indiscriminately chopping budgets, you might like to start by thinking about what business you're really in (see IDEA 43).

HOW ARE YOU DOING?

You've agreed on the plan that sets out what your customer's going to buy from you next year, and how you're going to go about meeting that demand (see IDEA 69).

The budget that expresses this plan in financial terms (putting a value on what your customers are going to buy, how much it's going to cost you to do the necessaries and hence how much money you're expecting to make) has finally been approved. Now you can get back to your 'proper job'... or perhaps not.

The idea

Your responsibility for financial planning does not stop once you've agreed on budgets.

A budget is not a licence to spend – it is just what is believed to be the best allocation of a scarce resource (money) to achieve the company's goals. It allows all the team players to work together in a co-ordinated approach understanding clearly which goal-mouth they're aiming for.

At a point in time.

Things don't always go according to plan. Not only do customers change their minds, costs also have an unnerving habit of spiralling out of control unless you keep a firm hand on them. You know your role in the team plan, what you've been tasked with achieving, and how much you're expected to need to spend in the process. Now you have to continually monitor your progress, both in what you're achieving and how much it's costing you.

Look ahead
Don't subscribe to the last minute school of management!

The best way to control costs and get the most you can from the money available is to be proactive rather than reactive.

Whenever materials have to be brought in at short notice or activities have to be rushed you can hear that shredding machine whirr into action as it eats up £50 notes from your (or very unfairly someone else's) budget – money that could have been used more effectively elsewhere. Suppliers have to be paid to lay on an extra shift, goods have to be freighted in (or out) at premium rates, you have to pay for unplanned overtime, people get stressed and make mistakes... (see IDEAS 22 & 90).

And that all costs money.

Squeeze value
Make sure every expenditure is properly authorised and negotiated to get the best value you can for every £1 you spend (see IDEA 13). If you are in control, the monthly summary of budgeted against actual spend should hold no surprises!

Don't stop planning
Setting a budget doesn't handcuff the business to what might turn out to be a sinking ship. If circumstances change, so must your plans. By monitoring and controlling how you're doing (and keeping your eyes and ears open), you should be able to pick up early indications of the need to recall the team and review your plans.

- Are you no longer able to fulfil your part of the plan?

- What impact will this have on the activities required by other team members?

- Do you need additional resources to deliver the activities that have been assigned to you? If so, can they be redistributed from savings made elsewhere? Or does the team need to revise the level of performance that can be achieved?

You are allowed to have good news as well as bad! Perhaps you have spotted an opportunity to win additional business and want to reconvene to discuss how you find the necessary funding to make this a reality. Or you might have been able to make savings on planned expenditure.

A possible remedy

This international pharmaceutical business reduces budgets when savings have been achieved to avoid the money disappearing on the budget holder's other activities. By 'clawing back' these savings they can then be offered up, if necessary, to meet potential overspends elsewhere in the organisation or, better still, used to support other profitable activities that had to be dropped from the original plans owing to lack of sufficient finance.

In practice

- Keep planning and get the best results from every £1 that you commit.

- Make sure all expenditure is authorised and has been professionally negotiated (see IDEA 13) and that your payroll costs are invested in activities that your customer is willing to pay for.

I COULD DO SOMETHING WITH THAT!

IS YOUR KITCHEN cupboard stuffed with ingredients that you bought for recipes you've long since lost or stopped making? Or ready-made meals that nobody wants?

Are these goods slowly edging their way towards their 'use by' dates so that, with great relief, you will be able to throw them out without too much of a guilty conscience?

The stores at work can be viewed on pretty similar lines.

The idea

Look for the equivalent of a back-to-front recipe book – one where you start by listing the ingredients you want to use up and are then given the recipe.

All too often there are components or final products in inventory that people would prefer not to use. The designer prefers to start afresh with a new approach. The salesman finds it much easier to sell the newest product in the range. How do you encourage them to use up these slow-moving less-attractive alternatives?

Bribery.

Let's face it. If we don't get someone to take these items off our hands they're going to end up in the skip. And that's effectively throwing away money. So there needs to be an incentive...

Commission-driven
The sales director of this company selling business equipment was frustrated by his regional managers' habit of trying to offload 'mature'

items into each others' warehouses to avoid being castigated for slow-moving inventory. (Some of these products were spending more time in transit than the sales managers were!) So he turned the shunned products into highly desirable items by initiating a multiplier effect on the commission they would earn – the harder to sell, the greater the commission. The idea initially worked a little too well as within days, his sales managers had over-sold the available stock of these previously troublesome lines!

Design for use
This manufacturing business supplies its designers with constantly updated schedules of 'bargain basement parts'. If the designer uses them, the project carries a fraction of the full cost – and the business saves the cost of buying a new part.

A variation on this theme…

Make it visual
Posted up in the design department of this business are photographs, descriptions, quantities and valuations for the slow-moving parts in store…

And whatever you do to use that slow-moving inventory, be careful not to end up with another funnel (see IDEA 96).

In practice

- Comb through the stores to identify those items that need to start moving and identify how you're going to encourage people to make them the inventory item of choice.

- Don't find yourself repeating the exercise in a few months time! You could start by looking at the benefits of standardisation (IDEA 46), shorter leadtimes through the business (IDEA 6) and whether you inadvertently encourage buyers to procure more than you need (see IDEA 30).

37 IF INVENTORY IS AN ASSET...

"IF INVENTORY IS an asset, why do we want to reduce it?"

A fair question.

The idea

By reducing the amount of cash you have locked up in inventory, you can reduce your loans (reducing the cost of interest) and/or reinvest in other business opportunities at no additional financial cost.

But this does not make for an easy life.

Dangerous waters

Most companies rely on holding inventory as a way of getting round short-comings in their performance. Hence inventory is often referred to as a 'sea of waste' used to cover the 'rocks' (business problems) beneath the surface. 'Rocks' such as late deliveries by suppliers, machine break-downs and scrap can be 'covered up' by having sufficient inventory in the system to avoid letting down the next person in the chain.

But who pays for this? Not your customer. The market will not pay a premium to suppliers who are incurring additional costs by continually turning a blind eye to their inefficiencies and failing to address problems lurking beneath the surface.

Depths of despair

The delegates to this in-house training program had unusually down-cast expressions. (OK, the thought of a day of financial training doesn't often engender excited anticipation, but this group were particularly glum.) Enquiring as to the reason for this, there followed an out-pouring of how the company had 'gone downhill' in the last year or so. Problems meeting delivery-schedules driven by shortages of materials, machine break-downs, products awaiting engineering concessions... the list was endless. Apparently such problems had never previously existed in the 25 years they had worked for the business. Smiling wryly, the trainer asked how much inventory had been taken out over the last 12 months. A substantial amount. The problems had always existed – it was just that previously they had been covered up by a sea of inventory.

Navigate carefully
Taking inventory out is a great way to identify 'rocks' – but be careful. There is only one person who brings cash into your business.

Your customer.

So you need to 'take the plug out' carefully making sure you don't allow deliveries to be jeopardised by grounding on the rocks.

Once you've 'blasted the top off your problem' you can then safely remove a bit more inventory... and so the process continues.

In practice

- Get the message out that despite what accountants say, inventory is not an asset but a risk (see IDEA 6).

- Understand why you have inventory in your business (see IDEA 96).

- Having identified the 'rocks' and getting to their root cause (see IDEA 27), start blasting!

INTERESTING THOUGHTS

MOST BUSINESSES HAVE to borrow money. When you borrow money, you bring an additional cost into the business – interest payments.

So how do you manage this cost?

The idea

How much interest you're going to have to pay will depend on how much you've borrowed and the rate of interest you're charged.

Release investment
The amount you need to borrow depends on how much you need in total to finance your business, less the amount that is supplied by shareholders as share capital or through reinvested profits. Therefore to reduce the amount you have to borrow, you need to focus on releasing any unnecessary money tied up in Fixed Assets and/or Working Capital.

There are plenty of great ideas elsewhere in this book about how to reduce the amount of money you have locked up in the business to release cash for, amongst other things, repaying some of that debt. If you need help getting started on finding the keys, take a look at IDEA 40.

But how can you negotiate the most favourable rates on your loans?

By keeping your lender onside.

A safe bet
In setting the rate, the lender will look to trade-off risk against

return; the greater the perceived risk, the higher the rate that will be set to 'reward' the lender for taking this risk.

So how do you convince your lender that you have everything under control and that you're a safe bet?

- **Be professional.**

  If you're going to convince him that your business will thrive you'll need a well-thought-through business plan. It's not enough just to explain your ideas, you're going to need to present the plan in financial terms as well. And remember that while everyone else might talk about profit, what the lender really wants to hear about is cashflow. (If you're not sure of the difference see IDEA 44.)

  While it's great to be positive, committed and up-bcat, it's a mistake to be overly optimistic. Present a plan that is realistic and impress your lender with having thought through the financial implications of possible up-sides and down-sides. Identify those factors that are critical to your success and look at the financial implications of them not going quite as planned.

  Show that you're organised by making sure you complete any documentation or fulfil requests for further information in a timely manner.

- **Keep your promises.**

  And if you can't –

- **Keep him informed.**

  Don't hide from him.

  If things are going awry, it's all the more reason to keep him on your side.

You're going to get a much better reception if you've worked out in advance that you're going to need a payment holiday, rather than just waiting for the call from the bank to warn you that you've reached your overdraft limit.

Knowing what's coming is a good sign that you understand your business – and that's something that your lender will appreciate.

In practice

* Work on your relationship with your lender and make an appointment with him to talk through your future plans.

INVOLVE EVERYONE

YES DESIGNERS, THAT includes you!

IDEA 43 looks at how important it is that designers (or those defining the service you provide) understand what customers are actually buying.

But when it comes to the question of how much the product or service will cost, it's important to remember that profit is not enough!

What is important is profitability – profit in relation to the amount of investment that had to be invested to earn that profit.

But what can matters of investment in land, buildings and machinery, relationships with suppliers, lead-times through the business, and credit periods to customers possibly have to do with designers?

The idea

Sustainable businesses need to design products or services that meet market needs not just in a cost-effective way, but that can also be delivered in an investment-efficient way.

Creating havoc
When running in-house financial awareness courses with delegates from across organisations, sessions often focus on the opportunities to reduce the amount of money tied up in the business (especially in Working Capital), while continuing to meet customer needs.

During the discussions it is explained that anyone who plays a part in the relationship with suppliers, the way products are made, and the relationship with customers will influence the amount of investment in Working Capital (see IDEA 40). If there is anyone in the session that doesn't have a role to play in any of these matters, you have to question why they're on the payroll. Most understand the impact they have. The one or two who believe that 'That's what everyone else does' usually turn out to be designers. Amidst wailing and gnashing of teeth, it is then pointed out that decisions made by designers have more influence on cost and the amount of investment that the company needs to make than anyone (or even possibly everyone) else in the room.

As soon as designers 'put pen to paper' they define the materials required and drive choices of manufacturing method. What you buy, who you buy from, and how things are made are fundamental to how much products cost and how much investment the business needs (see IDEA 97). But it may not just be designers...

Black holes

The same traits can be seen in others who may view their activities as 'off-line' to the flow of products through the business – you might find examples of this species in the habitats of those engaged in Quality Assurance and processing concessions. In a business where products are routed through these activities either for contractual reasons (batch testing) or because of short-comings (concessions), you may find there is ignorance of the implications working practices in these areas can have on those trying to plan activities downstream. And remember that where there is a problem, there's a cost (IDEA 90), and where there is pressure there's a hockey stick (IDEA 22)!

In practice

- Make sure every person understands that they work for the customer and that the sustainability of the business depends on meeting customer needs in a cost-effective way.

- Ask people to identify how they influence both cost and investment – and provide training where required.

40 IS YOUR WORKING CAPITAL WORKING?

WORKING CAPITAL IS a great bit of accounting jargon because it sets out quite clearly what we need to do with this investment – make it work!

The idea

Every £1 invested in the Working Capital cycle has had to come from somewhere – from shareholders who will want to be rewarded with dividends, or bankers who will want interest paid on their loans.

So you want as little Working Capital as possible while being able to keep your customers happy!

The cycle starts with cash.

DIAGRAM 1

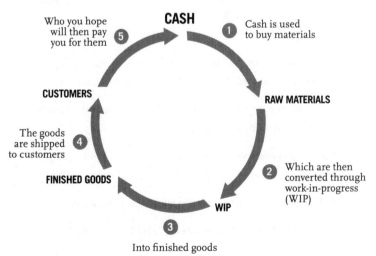

In reality, life is fortunately a little more complicated in that we rarely pay cash for materials. Instead, we have materials delivered to us and we then proceed to run as fast and furiously round the cycle to get as far as we can before we have to pay our suppliers. The further you get, the longer you are running on your supplier's money rather than your own.

DIAGRAM 2

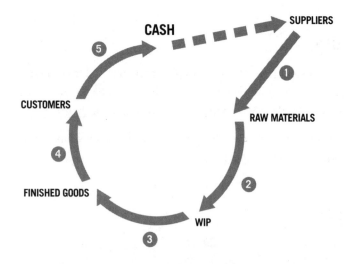

The amount of money you have tied up in raw materials, work-in-progress and finished goods is referred to as inventory (or stock).

The amount of money you are waiting to receive from your customers is known as receivables (or debtors).

The amount of money you owe your suppliers is known as payables (or creditors).

The investment in Working Capital therefore comprises:

(Inventory + Receivables + Cash) – Payables

How much Working Capital your business needs depends on how efficiently you manage the money you have tied up in inventory and receivables, and how well you have managed to offset this investment by the credit you have negotiated with suppliers (referred to as payables).

If you can release surplus investment you release cash – and you can use that cash to either get rid of some of those loans (thereby reducing the cost of interest payments) or to invest in other profitable business opportunities...

Finders keepers

This international group of companies allowed their subsidiaries free rein with the amount they spent on new plant and equipment (Capital Expenditure), on condition that it was self-funding from reducing their investment in Working Capital. A great motivation for companies to squeeze their Working Capital cycles to produce cash, re-invest it in those opportunities for business (and financial) growth, and effectively get something for nothing!

In practice

- Take a look at how much money your business has locked up in Working Capital – and then squeeze it! If you need some ideas to help you get started try IDEAS 95 & 96.

- It's no good if, behind your back, others are topping up the cycle faster than you can squeeze. Make sure everyone understands the impact their decisions have on the investment required – particularly those designers (see IDEA 97)!

41 IT FELL OFF THE BACK OF A LORRY

You've got the design. Now how are you going to make it?

Do you have the necessary skills in your workforce and the capability and capacity of your equipment to do it all yourself?

If not, how much work are you going to do in-house and which operations are going to be done at sub-contractors?

How much time does your product spend out on the open sea, on the motorway – or even on a fork-lift truck being carried round your site?

The idea

Choosing to off-load work brings additional costs into the business such as transportation and administration (see IDEA 89).

But of particular concern here is how routing the product in and out of the business will add to production lead times and therefore inventory values, interest costs and risk (see IDEA 37).

In addition, the more a product is transported around and handled, the greater the risk of damage and hence the cost of re-work or scrap (see IDEA 58).

Taken for a ride

The cross-functional improvement team in this business looked in bewilderment at the chaotic artwork in front of them. It was a site map on which they'd just plotted the journey taken by a troublesome component in the course of its manufacture. It travelled 4 miles back and forth around the 40-acre site and spent 98% of its time on a fork-lift or queuing for the next operation. They set to work.

6 months later, by eliminating or combining operations and improving manufacturing methods, they have taken 7 days out of the lead-time, reported a £200 reduction in product cost and taken £40,000 out of inventory.

And that's just phase 1 of the plan.

You can find 'speed' in surprising places.

Take the boxes emptied by shelf-stackers in supermarkets and then re-cycled. A manager from the packaging sector spoke of how fibres from one box can be reincarnated and back in store within 10 days. And they're not being complacent...

In practice

- Map the routes taken by your products.

- Identify the controls that have to take place (and hence costs that are incurred) every time a product changes location.

- Challenge production methods to reduce the number of 'handovers' and time spent in transit.

- Get designers to understand the consequence of their choices (see IDEA 97).

42 IT'S ALL A BIT OF A MUDDLE ...

SOME PEOPLE SEEM to prefer working in a muddle but this can be costly in terms of wasted time looking for things (especially in someone else's clutter) and create potentially expensive health and safety issues.

The idea

Create a work environment in which everything is to hand (and unnecessary items have been removed), allowing people to work efficiently and safely.

The process of establishing and maintaining such workspaces is often referred to as a '5C' (or '5S') event.

Step 1
Clearout (or Sort Out): Decide what is actually needed in the workplace and separate the essentials from the non-essentials. Non-essential items should then be re-housed as appropriate – e.g. back in the store, in a cupboard or in the bin.

Step 2
Configure (or Simplify): 'A place for everything and everything in its place'. Having taken into account the frequency and manner of use of the essential items, decide where they should be located. Shadowboards can be helpful in some instances.

Step 3
Clean and check (or Sweep): Having cleaned and tidied the area, agree how this is to be maintained and by whom.

Step 4
Conformity (or Standardise): Periodically repeat steps 1-3 to make sure the workplace condition is maintained and, even better, improved.

Step 5
Custom and Practice (or Self Discipline): Regular reviews are used to ensure every employee follows the agreed rules, understands the benefits, and contributes to the on-going improvement activities.

'De-cluttering' the workplace also complements other ideas in this book such as standardising the way tasks are performed (see IDEA 46) and preventing mistakes (see IDEA 27).

In the pink
To improve the probability of getting things 'right first time' by reducing the likelihood of incorrect use of parts, this manufacturer not only de-cluttered workspaces, but also colour-coded the work being done.

Each of the 5 product lines within the factory was allocated a colour, with common parts held in black containers. All paperwork, tooling and boxes containing product-specific parts were coloured accordingly. Now all workstations should not only be tidy but also be monotone – and the supervisor can see at a glance what product is being worked on.

In practice

- Ask around your networking group for recommendations for organisations that can help you kickstart the 5C (or 5S) process. There's often expertise (and even substantial financial help) to be found from government-sponsored organisations that support businesses in a given locality or within particular sectors

  (And when you've seen the benefits in the workplace you could turn your attention to your kitchen and garage...)

43 JUST WHAT THEY WANT – AND NO MORE!

In IDEA 81 and IDEA 94, it is explained how important it is to understand what exactly the customer wants and how much he is prepared to pay for a product or service with those attributes. Your task is then to align your business by organising yourself in such as way as to be able to deliver that product or service to the market at a profit.

The idea

If you build features into your offering that the customer doesn't want or doesn't value, you just build in unnecessary costs to your business. And if those unwanted features make the product more complex to make, or more complicated to use, or to maintain... all those £50 notes in the shredding machine (see IDEA 90).

That's money off the bottom line.

Don't forget to tell that to the designers (or those organising how the service is to be performed)!

It can be very informative to take a look at how your customer uses your product...

Think outside the box

A newly appointed Sales Manager to this pharmaceutical business decided to visit customers to see how they used the company's products. Imagine his surprise in seeing that the first thing this customer did was to rip open each of the carefully (and expensively) individually packaged items and tip them into a bulk dispensing unit for easy access. A great win-win opportunity to cut packaging and freight costs for the supplier and the customer's time and garbage costs.

But it doesn't stop there. Your customers' businesses are continually evolving – as must your offering if you are to continue to meet their needs.

Look to the future
Look for long-term relationships with your customers by supporting them not just by being world-class at doing what you've already been selected to do, but also by being pro-active in working with them to enable them to secure profitable new work.

Do you have good relationships with your customers? But who are those relationships with? Don't just woo the buyers! Keep in contact with the sales teams; visit sites on a regular basis to understand future plans for facilities and processes… and don't let their designers out of your sight!

In practice

- Don't do things your customer doesn't want and therefore isn't paying for.

- But do make sure that your customer pays for the value he's getting as every incremental £1 on price goes straight to profit.

- Ensure there is close dialogue between those talking to customers and the people designing your products or defining your service, and that these discussions don't just cover existing business but also explore opportunities for developing the partnership in the future.

- Remember that you are your customer's supplier – then ask yourself what you look for in a good supplier (see IDEA 18).

44 KEEP YOUR EYE ON THE TILL

PROFIT AND CASHFLOW are not the same thing.

And they don't even necessarily flow in the same direction.

Just because you make a profit doesn't mean you necessarily end up with more cash than you started with... and strangely you can make a loss and yet have more cash at the end than you had at the beginning.

The idea

Businesses don't go to the wall because they make losses – they fail because they run out of cash. Therefore it's really important to understand the difference between profit and cashflow, and hence the levers you have to pull to turn profit into cash.

Profit is measured by looking down the road. In calculating profit, your accountant compares the price that the customer is willing to pay for the goods you've shipped and the cost you've incurred in making them. The difference between the two is your profit. While this is a very useful piece of information, it's only one perspective on the business. For a fuller picture, the accountant needs to turn round and look at the business as a whole.

And that's where cashflow comes in.

(If you're not too sure how the Working Capital cycle works, you might find it helpful at this stage to take a look at IDEA 40 before reading on.)

Look back a couple of paragraphs at how that profit figure was calculated – and hence its limitations.

Profit takes account of what's gone out the door – but what has happened to the inventory levels in the business?

- If they've increased then you're tying up more cash.
- If they've decreased then you've released cash.

Profit takes account of what you've invoiced your customer – but what has happened to the total amount of cash you're waiting to collect (known as receivables or debtors)?

- If it has increased then you're tying up more cash.
- If it has decreased then you've released cash.

Neither does profit take account of what you've brought in from suppliers – but what has happened to the total amount you've currently got on credit from your suppliers (known as payables or creditors)?

- If it has decreased then you're tying up more cash.
- If it has increased then you've released cash.

(Be careful – this one is the other way round!)

And have you carried out any Capital Expenditure (i.e. bought any new Fixed Assets)?

Armed with the answers to those questions, you are in a position to understand what's happened (or better still, if you're looking at your plans, what's going to happen) to your cash.

Pull the levers

There are basically 5 levers you can pull to generate cash (other than going to the bank or the shareholders to borrow more and you can't keep doing that to get you out of trouble).

The levers are :

	Profit
Δ	**Inventory**
Δ	**Receivables**
Δ	**Payables**
	Capital Expenditure

and the way you pull them will determine your   **Cashflow**

(Δ is the increase or decrease in whatever you're measuring)

[If there are any accountants reading this book, don't get all hot around the collar about the definition of exactly which 'profit' we're talking about here or all those other twiddles you have to do to balance the figures to the penny... this isn't an accounting manual so let's just agree to focus on the message that matters and keep it simple. OK?]

Remembering the point made earlier that businesses fail because they run out of cash, can you see why you may want to take a look at those great ideas for how to manage your investment in stock, receivables, payables and new facilities and processes, as well as those focused on improving your profit?

In practice

- Unless your business model is very simple and you buy everything for cash, sell everything for cash, sell everything you buy each day and don't need any fixed assets, then profit and cashflow will not be the same thing.

- There is a saying that profit is vanity and cash is sanity – so planning your cashflow is even more important than planning your profit.

KEEPING EVERYONE FED AND WATERED

How MUCH IS it costing you to feed and water your workforce?

The cost of water-coolers is challenged in IDEA 1, but what about the other aspects of catering?

The idea

Check your catering arrangements.

Vending machines

Are you getting enough revenue from your coffee machines?

It's often perceived wisdom that vending machine profits are used to subsidise the canteen.

But are you actually making a profit?

Your vending machine maintenance costs may be more than you think. Just as with the water-coolers question, how many do you need to have? And how energy-efficient are they? While they might be a much better option than the kettles that were blowing the electricity tariff in one business (see IDEA 48), you may be surprised how much power old, inefficient machines can use.

Catering contracts

Is your canteen contractor complying with the contract and only charging allowable expenses? In typical contracts the company provides and maintains the kitchen equipment, pays a management charge to the catering company, and covers the utilities. Revenue from the canteen is usually expected to cover the cost of the food.

Does your contract state who covers the cost of stand-in labour in the case of sickness? Who is responsible for selecting, negotiating and ordering the equipment for the kitchen? Is the contractor measured and therefore motivated to manage utility usage?

Restaurant facilities
Don't overlook the opportunity to make other improvements in the restaurant as well.

As people clear away, have them use specific recycling bins where possible. This will reduce your costs for waste removal – and make the catering task easier and therefore less costly.

Put items such as serviettes and sauces at the checkout to prevent customers from taking more than they need.

Catered meals
And what about food that is eaten away from the restaurant?

What arrangements do you have for providing meals for meetings?

A team of PAs from across this business were tasked with reviewing the catering arrangements. Amongst other issues they found that there were no controls in place over who could order food for working lunches.

Looking back over the records for recent months, it was surprising how many people had had to arrange meetings over lunchtime. Not only this, but there were no controls over the menus or quantities offered. The food supplied tended to be unhealthy and the billing from the catering company suspect.

Given that the catering company would be reimbursed for any food served there was little incentive for them to be cost-conscious. On the contrary, there was every reason to off-load as much food as possible whenever possible – particularly if they could use up products nearing the end of their shelf-life!

The company has now implemented a proper authorisation process for catered meetings. Menu options have been formalised and quantities specified – a healthy option all round!

In practice

- Work out how much (and where) you spend money on feeding and watering your staff – it's effectively part of your payroll costs.

- How much of this is on automated vending? Question how many machines you need and the costs and revenues involved.

- Catering contracts (like cleaning contracts – see IDEA 67) need to be clearly specified with defined measures of performance – and agreed sanctions to be applied should the standards not be met.

46 KEEPING UP STANDARDS

Unless you specialise in 'one-off' creations, your customers are going to expect consistency in the features and quality of repeat purchases.

How can you consistently replicate quality products and thereby reduce the costs of customer rejects and warranty claims?

By reducing variability in the materials you buy and the processes you use.

Your choice of supplier and the nature of your partnership will influence your ability to ensure materials are of a consistent quality (see IDEA 18).

But what about your processes?

Have you selected equipment that has the capability of producing a consistent outcome – and has it been maintained properly?

Does everyone carry out the tasks required in the same way?

The idea

You need to have standardised processes not just for quality purposes but also to facilitate training and prevent the expensive consequences of single-point failure (see IDEA 77). To select the best methods you need your experts – the people carrying out the work on a regular basis.

This is a great opportunity not just to identify the best way to carry out the task but also to get more people engaged in improvement activity, allowing you to tap into all that latent knowledge lying beneath the management surface.

Phographic evidence

The manager of this business gets all the experts together and explains the job at hand – to determine the best way to carry out a specific task so that a quality product is produced every time, using a method that is efficient, effective and transferable through training. He then hands over a video camera and steps back, leaving his experts to get on with it. Once the proposed method is agreed on and accepted it is videoed for training purposes, photographed for use as visual workplace instructions – and monitored to make sure it is being adhered to.

So much for your existing products – but what about new products?

Learn from experience

Are designers encouraged to adapt proven tried and tested designs wherever practicable, and actively discouraged from re-inventing the wheel every time they have the opportunity?

Do they have feedback from production with regard to the relative ease of quality manufacture for each product?

Do salesman regularly brief designers about problems found out in the field?

Do designs reflect a clear understanding of just what the customer wants – and no more (see IDEA 43)?

Not only does standardisation of design approach potentially ease the journey through the financially challenging stage of product introduction (see IDEA 97); the standardisation of materials can also reduce costs in other ways.

Common sense

The greater the commonality of parts, the lower the risk of obsolescence.

With fewer variants, higher volumes of standard parts will allow buyers opportunities to negotiate volume discounts.

Fewer part numbers may mean fewer suppliers and fewer purchase orders, thereby reducing the costs of procurement.

With commonality of parts, overall stockholding can be reduced, releasing cash for other purposes.

With fewer parts in stock, the area of the stores can be reduced to free up space.

And while your final products may look very different, there may be opportunities to standardise up to a point... (see IDEA 25).

In practice

- Look for opportunities to standardise designs and methods – this should help reduce both investment and risk.

- Remind your designers of the importance of avoiding branded items in their specifications, as it significantly reduces the opportunity for buyers to negotiate better deals.

- Find opportunities to remove complexity from other aspects of your business as complexity breeds cost (see IDEA 20).

47 KEEPING YOUR DOGS UNDER CONTROL

When demand for your product starts to fall as it reaches the last stage of its demand life-cycle, it is referred to as a 'dog' (see IDEA 64). If you've avoided being a lemming, you've predicted the cliff-edge and controlled your stock levels by keeping in pace with customer demand. You've now got to realign the way you manage this product or service through your business to control the costs.

The idea

What may have been the best process for making the product in an earlier stage may not be so appropriate now that as a 'dog', it is demanded less frequently and/or in smaller quantities.

Round them up

A manufacturer of small but relatively high-value products segregated manufacture between two sites. One site dealt with the high-volume repeaters in the 'cow' stage of life while the other produced the 'strangers and aliens' associated with the 'dog' stage. Equipment was aligned to needs with the emphasis on cost-effective high volume machinery for the former and equipment enabling fast changeovers for the latter.

When customers came to 'help them take cost out of their products' it was important to plan the visit to make sure that they steered the customer firmly towards the 'dogs' and away from the 'cows' (see IDEA 80).

Selective breeding

Another manufacturer looked at not only how he could realign the type of equipment used to make his product, but also how he could merge orders by standardising the product wherever possible and leaving the differentiated packaging as far downstream the process as he could.

Sting in the tail

When checking out the condition of your 'dogs', remember that your costing system might not pick up on those additional 'hassle' costs brought about by the complexity of producing small quantities of a large range of items (see IDEA 26).

In practice

- Look critically at the condition of your 'dogs' and be selective about which ones you keep.

- Manage the demise of those to be discontinued to avoid being left with obsolete stock on the shelf.

KILLER WATTS

IF YOU'RE GOING to improve on the cost of your utilities, you need to tackle not just the amount you use (see IDEA 4) but also the price you pay.

The idea

Check your bills.

Energy consultants say that this is often the quickest way of reducing costs! Errors on utility bills are apparently rife. It's hard enough having to pay what's due. Check that the amount you've used has been correctly calculated and charged before authorising the payment.

You may be able to make savings by rescheduling or re-engineering activities.

Save on charges

It's common knowledge that it's wasteful to leave mobiles etc. on charge overnight without either a timer or a device to cut-off when the battery is fully loaded. But do you remember that when you charge or recharge more sizeable batteries?

A member of the training department in this international business returned from visiting the shopfloor and asked how the fork-lift trucks were powered. When she was told they used rechargeable batteries, she asked when the charging took place and whether this coincided with the lowest tariff. So simple and yet nobody had thought about it. Of course this led to discussions on the use of timers or cut-off devices... and the interesting revelation that the company paid more than 9 different tariffs throughout the working week.

Get off that peak

Tariffs may depend on peak usage so find out what lies behind those times of maximum demand.

For the people running this factory, it surprisingly came down to a question of boiling point.

The tariffs for the company's electricity costs were banded according to usage. Bills showed that the trigger-point for the maximum rate was being exceeded every working day. Was it when the heating (or air-conditioning) systems kicked in early in the morning? Was it when everyone arrived and turned on equipment? No. It was at lunchtime when hundreds of kettles were plugged in. The solution? Hot-water heaters in the kitchen areas – and a ban on kettles.

In practice

- Check those bills!

- Collect information on how much power you use, what it's used for, and importantly, when you use it.

- Understand the tariff structure for your business and communicate it to others. Manage your costs by identifying power-intensive tasks that could be scheduled for low-tariff slots.

  (Tariffs can be exceedingly complicated. Don't baffle people with masses of numbers. Present the tariff in terms of red and green time zones... while reminding everyone that it would be better still if they could avoid using the power at all!)

MAKE SURE YOU'RE NOT INADVERTENTLY INCREASING COSTS!

How INTEGRATED IS the management of your business? Do you have 'joined up' thinking by your management team? Or are metrics (or measures of performance) departmentalised with scant regard as to whether great performance in one area has struck a blow elsewhere?

You get what you measure – so make sure it's what you want (see IDEA 10).

The idea

Look carefully at proposals to improve costs as not all of them will have the desired effect.

Purchasing savings

Keep your purchasing staff close to their customers – that is, everyone else in the business. Be cautious of making price savings the key performance target for buyers as this might prove to be a very costly improvement initiative! What matters isn't price but value, so you need to monitor usage to see if you're really saving money. Whenever buyers change the source or specification of products not only should they review the impact on usage, but they should also check with their internal customers for feedback on other cost impacts.

For example, if you change your supply of materials you need to consider not just the effect on usage but also issues such as whether machines jam more frequently, assembly takes longer, or if there are increases in warranty claims. Purchasing cheaper paper for your printer may not just mean you can no longer duplex print, but the dust produced may mean more frequent service call-outs...

Total acquisition costs

Side-stepping suppliers approved by headoffice for cheaper alternatives might result in the overall loss to the group of retrospective purchasing discounts.

Buying more expensive (but more energy-efficient) equipment may prove the cheaper option. And don't overlook other types of running cost – for example, the lower-priced printer might require expensive print cartridges.

Personnel

The total acquisition cost of your most valuable assets – your people, is phenomenal. Just think payroll into perpetuity! So it might pay to re-think what constitutes cost-effective when it comes to the selection and remuneration of employees.

And of course there are those decisions taken to 'save money' by sub-contracting work out – where you end up paying the supplier's costs as well as your own (see IDEA 89).

And investing in tooling to save time making your products only to find that you haven't actually saved any money... in fact, you've added to your costs by buying the tooling (see IDEA 98).

'Make do and mend' may be costing you a fortune (see IDEA 79).

It's not that straight-forward is it?

In practice

- Talk through the wider implications of cost improvement proposals with all parties before implementation – then monitor and review to pick up on any unintended consequences. These might not always be negative!

50 MANAGING EXPECTATIONS

IF YOU'RE HEADING up cost improvement activities in your organisation, have you ever felt like Superman?

Or rather have you ever felt that others saw you as Superman... and then got very disillusioned when the veil fell from their eyes?

The idea

There is often an unrealistic expectation about just how much (and importantly, how quickly) financial benefit can be gained from improvement activities.

Temperatures rise when, despite great cost improvement activities, managers are unable to find the benefit 'on the bottom line'. Distrust of the accountant's 'numbers' follows, communication breaks down, and improvement teams start generating their own version of costing information until there are duplicated systems without any hope of reconciliation...

The harsh reality is that while some improvement activities will benefit your cash position (e.g. collecting the cash faster from your customers), some will benefit your profit and your cash (e.g. buying in kits rather than parts, thereby releasing floorspace so that you no longer have to rent that storage space), but some will bring no financial benefit whatsoever (e.g. reducing the time to make a product or deliver a service when you have no productive work to fill the released capacity). In the short term.

While they don't bring any immediate financial benefit to the business, this last category of improvements do present an opportunity. An opportunity to do something valuable (i.e. something that the customer values and will pay for) with that released capacity on the machine, or that released workload for an employee or that released floorspace.

Which is why I like to refer to them as 'enablers'.

And encourage them.

And suggest you identify the cost of them separately on your financial reports so that management see that it is their responsibility to take action, and 'follow through' to seize the financial benefit by either finding that productive work, or down-sizing the business to release the cost.

In practice

- Manage expectations by being realistic about the financial benefits of activities.

- Identify whether a planned activity should improve profit and/or cash, the anticipated financial value of the improvement, and the timescale in which this should be achieved.

- Re-engineer your reporting to segregate the cost of 'enablers', focusing management attention on the opportunity to reap that reward.

51 MAVERICKS AND OTHER CHALLENGING PERSONALITIES

You MAY HAVE considered the skills and talents required by your workforce when recruiting – but how do their personalities contribute to the cost improvement process?

The idea

Watch your mavericks. While you may value their unique capabilities it may be costing you dearly. Rottweilers pose a different challenge and carriers are contagious.

Mavericks
Mavericks tend not to be too good at co-operating and communicating. The maverick salesman may well bring in more business than anyone else – but is it the business that you want? Or can afford?

- Does he sell 'solutions' before he has checked if you have products that meet the customer's demands and specifications?

- Is he a 'big picture' person who pays little attention to detail – such as the payment terms?

- Does he have 'special relationships' with customers so that paperwork is brushed aside leaving you with uncollectable invoices (see IDEA 70)?

- Does he tend to take orders and leave other people to worry about whether there is the capacity to fulfil them? And if somehow capacity can be found, at what cost to the business? Will the apparent margin cover the cost of disruption (and consequent mistakes), overtime, premium charges from suppliers, delays to other orders...?

- Does he take orders you just can't afford (see IDEA 76)?

Maverick designers can come up with some wonderful designs – but will they make you money?

It's no point designing a product or service the market doesn't want. And if the market does want it, has the designer worked closely with the people responsible for making the product to ensure that the design will not just deliver profit, but that consideration has also been given to the amount of investment required – and hence the issue of profitability?

- Does he like to re-invent the wheel each time rather than use standardised solutions where possible (see IDEA 46)?

- How good is he at the 'unglamorous' aspects of the job – such as providing the technical documentation to accompany the product, without which the invoice will remain unpaid?

Rottweilers

Rottweilers, on the other hand, can make a great contribution to improvement activities.

While such people may not be the easiest of companions at times, their unwillingness to let things go makes them very effective at finding the root cause of problems (see IDEA 27).

And it's useful to have influential friends...

Carriers

Having experienced the benefits of an organisation switched-on to 'waste-busting', this manager started by identifying the 'carriers' in his business – those key individuals who have a disproportionate impact on business culture because of their ability to affect and influence behavioural norms and attitudes to work. Even if to date they may have been amongst the least-persuaded by his arguments he knew that the greatest (and often most vocal) objectors can, if converted, become the greatest advocates.

In practice

- Spot the mavericks around you and weigh up the benefits they bring, against the costs you may have to incur 'fixing' the problems they tend to leave in their wake.

- Check that every improvement team has a rottweiler.

- Find out who are the 'carriers' in your organisation and make an effort to bring them on-board.

52 MILK THOSE COWS!

PRODUCTS OR SERVICES that have gone through the development stage, have been introduced into the market, and for which there is now relatively stable demand are known as 'cows' – or more importantly, as 'cash cows' (see IDEA 64). As it says on the label, if you get it right, you can milk the 'cow' and cash should pour back into the business.

The idea

Nurture your 'cows' to ensure a high cash yield through their ability to earn decent margins on reducing investment.

There are two reasons why you should be earning decent margins on your products. Firstly, if you've aligned your business correctly and understood what your customer wants, the price he is currently paying 'rewards' you not just for the ongoing costs you are incurring, but also for the investment you've already made in the earlier development and 'star' stages of the cycle. Secondly, as you've tackled a lot of those teething problems (e.g. with tooling) that had previously been adding to your costs, your margins improve.

Not only do margins look good, investment in Working Capital should also be decreasing as you can reduce buffer stock as sales volumes and lead times become more predictable and your supply chain and quality more reliable.

However, businesses have a strange habit of killing off their cows.

It's often the fault of the costing system. Absorption costing systems tend to over-cost products at the 'cow' stage of the cycle (see IDEA 26).

Does this matter? It does if people unwittingly use the costing system for decision-making. Operations are moved to sub-contractors as the 'make-buy' decision gets distorted; products are moved to 'low-cost' economies that aren't; and if prices start to fall due to increased competition, the decision is taken to axe products that are in reality still highly profitable.

Job lot

This sub-contractor offered two capabilities – high-tech machining and manual assembly – but unfortunately had only one internal cost rate. The effect of this was to substantially under-cost what were cost-intensive machining jobs and over-cost assembly work. At a strategic review, they looked at the financials and decided to ditch their assembly work on which they appeared to be making little if any margin and canvass for loads more apparently highly-profitable machining work. The result? Disastrous. It became all too clear that the assembly work was their cash cow and that without it the business, from a financial standpoint, began to grind to a halt. The company did survive but had a tough time with huge amounts of debt to service while it reversed its strategy and focused on what actually proved to be not only its cash cow, but also its core competence – manual assembly.

In practice

- Manage your products through each stage of their life-cycle – you may need to squeeze every drop you can out of your 'cows' if you're going to be able to find the cash to bring those new products to fruition.

- Treat the information from your costing system with scepticism (see IDEA 26)!

NOT THAT AGAIN!

CONCESSIONS.

THESE ARE supposed to be that rare event when a part you are making fails inspection but is potentially salvageable. The engineer examines the part and decides that it is either fit-for-purpose as it is, or issues re-work instructions or declares it as scrap.

The idea

Eliminate (or at least start to tackle) the causes of concessions.

Before you go any further, let's think about the cost you're incurring when raising concessions. Not just the cost of the materials and labour that you've spent getting the product to this stage if it ends up in the skip, but the cost of the engineer's time in dealing with the concession, the cost of any re-work – and the cost of having disrupted the flow through the shopfloor.

Imagine 6 people standing in a line with a supply of cabbages at one end. Every time the bell rings cabbages are thrown to the next person down the line with the final 'customer' waiting at the end. All is well until someone (let's call him John) drops their cabbage i.e. raises a concession. While John is on the floor scrabbling to retrieve his cabbage the person before him on the line, unaware of his problem, keeps lobbing cabbages in his direction while those further downstream are cabbage-less. Grabbing an armful of cabbages, our butter-fingered catcher John then chucks three cabbages at a time to the person next-in-line who, unable to deal with them all at once...

Chaos.

No poetry in motion here then (see IDEA 55).

Where you get chaos you get waste. And where you get waste you get cost.

So it's agreed. Concessions are disruptive and expensive.

So you would never raise the same concession twice – would you?

It all adds up

Engineers in this business analysed the work they did on concessions. The problem was the work they didn't do. Armed with the information that it cost the company £500 to deal with each concession, they proceeded to automatically scrap off any part with a value of under £500 without entering it into the concession process. So parts valued at under £500 that came in time after time weren't included in the analysis and didn't get what was, in many cases, a simple 'fix'.

In practice

- Analyse concessions and look for repeaters.

- Get to the root cause of why they are happening and fix it. Permanently.

- Even if there is no pattern of repeated part numbers, look for repeated themes. Could the problem lie with a particular process? A particular individual? A particular supplier?

NOW YOU'RE ROLLING!

SOME IMPROVEMENT ACTIVITIES don't seem to improve the finances very much. In fact, some improvement activities don't improve the finances at all.

At least not immediately.

But that doesn't mean to say you shouldn't encourage everyone to continue to generate the opportunities these 'enablers' offer (see IDEA 50).

The idea

Even if your improvement activity has delivered a financial benefit, don't think 'job done' as this might be just the starting point for what's out there for grabs.

Take the example of what you can achieve by reducing inventory.

Taking out inventory is usually a positive thing to do as it releases cash to either get rid of some debt, or to reinvest in a great opportunity elsewhere in the business.

But don't stop there! This is just the tip of the iceberg!

Never let it be said that a once-off release of cash isn't worth having, but taking inventory out can do far more for you than just that.

By reducing the amount of inventory you hold, you begin to see the wood for the trees and spot other improvement opportunities.

If you're not holding as much inventory, you won't be using so much space or need so much store activity...

When this company reduced the amount of inventory they were holding, they used the opportunity to free-up floorspace which they then sub-let to a key supplier who could then deliver his product straight on to the production line as and when required. This saved purchasing, expediting and receiving costs and the space they would have required to store this large component which then allowed them to...

Can you see how you can start to roll?

In practice

- View improvement activities as starting points and begin to roll out the benefits.

55 **POETRY IN MOTION!**

How OFTEN DO you choose the wrong queue? This isn't necessarily because of the idiosyncrasies of the people in front of you, but a question of how the service has been organised and is being delivered and is more about movement than hard work.

The idea

Don't just focus on how hard people are working – look at *what* they're doing.

When it comes to working out the way a task should be done in the workplace, it can be a great idea to allow the people who do the task to video each other and then agree on the best method for doing that specific job. Videos can be made for training purposes and a manual prepared using photographs to explain the step-by-step process (see IDEA 46).

If the workplace is disorganised there's going to be wasted time looking for things (see IDEA 42).

If people have to walk around collecting the tools and materials they need to do the job, there's going to be wasted movement.

If there are activities that are being done unnecessarily...

Basket case
The new assembly supervisor watched his operator unpack components from a number of different containers and prepare them as kits. Examining the containers, he noticed that all the main parts came from one supplier with a handful of other minor parts coming from various sources. Here was an opportunity for

improvement. Why couldn't the main supplier deliver all the parts together as a kit? The supervisor then watched as the operator took each kit and loaded it into a specially designed basket ready for cleaning – an essential first-step in the assembly process. Now the supervisor was ready to take his idea to his manager!

Kits are now delivered directly to the assembly area in their baskets ready for washing. When the supplier delivers he collects the empty baskets for the next round of deliveries.... and there's now the opportunity to use the baskets as a signal to the supplier of how many kits are required!

In practice

- Just as you should trace the route taken by products to reduce lead times (see IDEA 41) so too should you consider the actions required to complete tasks.

- Map task journeys on a plan of the site and measure the distances covered – in extreme cases try experimenting with pedometers!

PRINTING MONEY

WHEN ASKING AROUND for ideas on how to improve business costs, it was astonishing how many people went straight for advice on controlling printing costs.

Of course these costs can be significant.

One manager found that for the 350 people they had on site, there were a total of 113 printers and copiers costing £80,000 in maintenance and cartridge costs alone.

Can you beat that?

The idea

Here are some of the suggestions made.

What steps can you take?
Well, this was the most common advice given: as many as possible.

The further away the printer is located, the more people will think twice before printing something.

Centralise your printers – and issue hiking boots to those needing to print in colour. If the 'confidentiality' card is being played, go for printers that require a user-entered PIN code to print documents held in a queue.

To reduce usage...
Tell people what it costs to copy and print (see IDEA 71) and then charge them.

Display the number of copies made that day on a large screen near the printer.

Have people question printing as the preferred solution – take a look at the creative approach used by the party animal in IDEA 21. If you enable users to scan direct to e-mail it saves printing costs – and postage!

Train people how to use the printers – especially when doing reductions or enlargements. Then, as with the shopfloor (see IDEA 46), use visual aids to remind people of the process. (If you're not sure this is necessary, try putting a paper recycling bin next to the machine for a while. You might be surprised how quickly it fills.)

Beware the print button on interactive boards.

Have a clear policy on the use of printers for personal business.

To encourage cost-effective choices...
A local college produces a list of printing costs by person to be charged against the relevant departmental budget... except for printing done on the lowest cost-per-copy centralised machine.

Set defaults to black and white duplex copies. (One contributor suggested 4 pages per sheet but that may be excessive if you don't have great eyesight!)

To keep within her budget, this headteacher, knowing her staff's enthusiasm for colour copies, limits them to a fixed number in any one year. Instead of automatically reaching for the colour button, they now think twice.

Hide coloured paper. (It may look attractive, but it's much more expensive!)

Would it be cheaper to use local printers for high-volumes? If so, encourage people to make this choice by limiting the numbers of copies that can be printed at any one time and having a simple process in place for placing orders with the selected supplier. This hospital physiotherapy department used to photocopy the blank forms used for patient notes. Now these forms are ordered automatically from the local printer at a fraction of the cost. Of course it is important to consider how frequently the form changes and not to end up with unusable stock in the stationery store... (see IDEA 30).

To reduce the cost per printed page...
Reduce the resolution on the printer to use less ink.

Look for cheaper sources of supply for paper and cartridges. Can you use refilled cartridges?

Use lighter paper – perhaps 60gm or 70gm instead of 80gm for internal documents? But be careful that you don't inadvertently increase costs if the machine jams more often.

Consider carefully the warranty and service agreement requirements on the equipment. Try to identify the source of branded items – if nothing else, it will arm you for the next contract review.

In practice

- Talk to people about how much money your business spends in total on printing and copying.

- Put visual displays over every printer and copier stating the cost per page, and directing people towards alternative lower-cost options.

- Encourage everyone to pause before pressing the button and ask:

  - Do I really need to print this?

  - If I do, what is the cheapest option open to me?

  - How can we improve the process so that in future I don't!

57 PROCESSES NOT PARISHES

YOUR TEAM DOESN'T work for a department, they work for the customer. Only the customer brings cash into the business as he pays for the products or services that he values.

The idea

Businesses that have strong departmental boundaries run the risk of limiting improvements to those making departments run more smoothly, rather than those that smooth the flow of activities to meet customer demands in the most cost-effective way possible.

If departmental loyalties are paramount, enhanced performance in one department may be detrimental to another's – such as the buying department making purchase price savings, only for these to be wiped out by the additional cost of scrap incurred by the manufacturing department as a result of poor quality materials (see IDEA 49).

Managing costs on a departmental basis may also risk overlooking opportunities for savings. It can be useful to look across the business at categories of spend. In isolation, departmental costs for e.g. photocopying may not appear significant. But add up the expenditure for the site and there's a situation worthy of attention.

If departments fail to work closely together, they may be busily wasting their time producing information that nobody wants, or even worse than that...

Double trouble
During a training program in a large multinational business, the

discussion moved to the concept of internal customers. Delegates were asked to form cross-departmental groups and select one person within the group for whom they would develop a diagrammatic illustration of their internal information suppliers, what they did with the information supplied, and their internal customers for this information. A heated debate started in one corner of the room. Investigation showed that two people working for completely different departments were producing the same information (even more worryingly in two completely different ways) for the same customer. What a waste!

In contrast, this manufacturing business looks to maximise the benefits from improvement suggestions by making sure the opportunities they throw up are considered beyond the confines of just one department.

Ripple rewards

To achieve this cross-fertilisation, each suggestion is reviewed by the immediate manager together with heads from two completely different departments who will both be asking, "Is there anything in this for us?" (A further advantage of this arrangement is that providing two fresh sets of eyes should deter suggestions being dismissed out of hand with the words, "That's not how we do it here." – see IDEA 2)

In practice

- Find out about process mapping and then have a go at a simple process in your business that will require you to cross departmental boundaries.

- Don't forget to involve everyone who plays a part in the process you're checking out and encourage them to challenge the status quo.

PRODUCING RUBBISH

What's the point of all that effort making things for them to end up in the skip? You may as well just drop £50 notes into a shredding machine (see IDEA 90).

The idea

To reduce the cost of scrap, you need to identify and tackle the root cause of why it's happening in your business.

Many things can influence how much scrap you have.

- If your designers pay little heed to the reality of the technical capability of processes, you may have components that you or your suppliers struggle to make to specification and assemblies that don't pass test.

- If your workforce is not trained, skilled and provided with the right tools and information to do the job, how likely are they to get it 'right first time'?

- If your equipment and tooling isn't properly maintained, what chance is there of making the product to the required tolerance?

- How far does your product travel and how often does it get handled (see IDEA 41)?

A flawed process
A components manufacturer identified a 5% scrap rate on a precision welded part. Checking the routing he found that the component was delivered free of charge to a sub-contractor who would perform

the welding operation and then return the part to the company. The part would then be inspected and, if rejected, scrapped off. However the sub-contractor was paid regardless of whether his work was subsequently scrapped-off or not. Not much incentive there! Once he had been told that he would not be paid for faulty work the scrap rate miraculously dropped to 0.5%.

And be careful what you do with your scrap.

More than he'd bargained for
This manager from an aerospace components manufacturing business was surprised to find one of the company's products at a car boot sale. While it emerged that the product had been scrapped off and the item removed from a skip, the company had to undergo a costly investigation from the aviation authorities for not putting reject goods clearly beyond serviceable use.

In practice

- Make sure that scrap is properly recorded – you can't manage what you don't know about.

- Get to the root cause of scrap – and fix it.

- Remember that your scrap may have a value (see IDEA 11) – so don't let it walk!

READ CAREFULLY

It's THERE IN the small print – but did you read the document carefully before signing up? Do you really understand what you are letting yourself in for? The agreement may be far more costly than you'd anticipated.

The idea

Check your procedures for taking orders and approving purchases.

Supplier contracts
In a rush to seal the deal with your supplier, did you check all the details about your purchase before committing?

Is there a precise specification and are the appropriate quality measures agreed (see IDEA 67)?

Is the delivery time acceptable? Are there minimum order quantities? Who is responsible for the cost of freight?

Customer contracts
Of course you checked the price... didn't you (see IDEA 70)? But have you checked the basis for escalations (see IDEA 66) or the commitment to year-on-year price decreases?

In the excitement of winning the order did you check out those terms and conditions properly before signing up?

What are the payment terms?

Did you check that the proposed delivery schedule to the customer was achievable?

Who carries the cost of shipping and insurance?

And of course you made sure you understood the precise product specification requirements... didn't you?

A chilling tale

The engineering department of this organisation had been working closely with their customer over some months on a new product. Details of the design and required capability of this technologically challenging component had been the subject of lengthy discussions. Drawings were prepared and accepted. Contracts were signed. Congratulations given.

When the first component was delivered to the customer some months later, it was rejected because it had not undergone the required test procedure. On re-examination of the contract, the engineer found to his horror that it stated that testing was to be done at -55° not the -45° he remembered from the earlier discussions. This proved to be an expensive problem to resolve. With no facilities available locally to carry out the test to this specification, the product had to be shipped overseas for testing at a cost of $100,000. The test results were disappointing as materials respond differently at lower temperatures...

In practice

- Are all your purchases properly authorised?

- Do you have a checklist for use prior to authorisation?

- Take a look at the controls in place over order intake.

- Just as with purchasing, do you have a proper procedure for reviewing contracts before taking on new business?

- A fresh set of eyes might be helpful (see IDEA 2).

SINGLE POINT FAILURE

WATCH OUT FOR potential single-point failure in your business – where there is a critical operation for which only one person has the required knowledge or expertise.

The idea

There's a problem if any step in your process of getting work out of the door and invoiced to the customer depends on the skills of one person.

Sometimes you're at the mercy of the customer as this business was when it was unable to despatch and invoice goods until they had been approved by an elusive source inspector (see IDEA 85).

Sometimes the problem is of your own making...

Beware the operator with the 'magic touch'.

Spelling trouble

An engineering business found itself a victim in several ways. Firstly at production meetings, the newly appointed operations manager noticed an interesting seasonal variation in the backlog of orders for a specific range of products. Further questioning elicited the reason why this correlated very closely with the holiday patterns of a single operator (let's call him Fred) out on the shopfloor.

Fred was the only one who could carry out a particularly tricky process and so all products requiring this operation would be put on one side while he was away on holiday, awaiting his return. Because of the power he therefore wielded, supervisors were wary of upsetting him and he had a vested interest in perpetuating the situation by not imparting his 'trade secrets'.

The solution? Firm supervision, enforced cross-skilling... and a discussion with the design team about the cost impact of products designed to incorporate such a tricky process!

The second instance involved a machine purchased second-hand from a closure sale of a local business. Now making some of the closing business' product lines, the machine looked a perfect fit for both the products transferred and others in the range and came highly recommended by an operator who had coincidentally worked on the machine in a previous employment. What became clear over the months of frustration that followed was that the company had failed to procure a vital part of the process – the one individual who had perfected the art of setting up the highly productive, but highly temperamental, machine.

In practice

- Track down your single-points and start cross-training.

- Locate emergency back-up support for specialist skills – as did the manager in IDEA 31.

61 SPARE A THOUGHT

BUSINESSES OFTEN CLAIM to make great margins on their spares. They might well do so but sometimes they overlook the impact of customers wanting 'one-offs'.

The idea

When judging products by their margins, make sure you're picking up all the costs. Take this example:

A customer orders a spare part at a price of £10. The manufacturer buys the complete part in from a supplier who charges £4 but has a minimum order quantity of 5. If the manufacturer receives the 5 parts into stock and ships one of them out to the customer, the chances are that the reported profit margin will be £6 (or 60%). But what if those remaining 4 parts are never required and are eventually disposed off as obsolete stock? Does anyone report back that the margin on the sale was really a loss of £10?

It's a great idea to check through your spare parts list to see which items are affected by minimum order quantities from suppliers and whether normal spares order volumes cover these without having to hold too much stock.

Where this isn't the case, decide whether it is appropriate to:

- put minimum quantities on sales of those parts, or

- increase the selling price to cover some or all of the cost of the potentially obsolete items, or

- if it is commercially unacceptable to do either of the above, write-off the excess items as they come in so that the margin report shows clearly that this is not the kind of business you want to promote!

Note that in the above example even though you may have to pay for all 5 items, you don't necessarily have to receive them. If they're just going to gather dust and occupy floorspace until they're eventually written off... there may be better ways to use that space (see IDEA 63)!

There are also plenty of other additional costs to think about associated with managing spares where there tends to be lots of orders for different parts in small quantities – the complexity of purchasing, production scheduling, and despatching activities for a start.

Does your costing system pick up on this (see IDEA 26)?

If not, just as Mark Twain said that the reports of his death were greatly exaggerated... so might your spares margins.

In practice

- Look critically at your reported spares margins and ascertain where you're really making money.

- Identify the steps you need to take to turn loss-makers into profit-earners, and for the rest, plan an exit-strategy to avoid leaving obsolete stock on the shelf.

62 SPENDING TIME...

J‌UST AS IT's important to be clear on personal use of business property (see IDEA 68), it's also important to send out a clear message that it should be company business in company time.

The idea

There needs to be a consistent approach taken by the management team on issues such as time-keeping, coffee breaks and personal phone calls, with everyone aware of the disciplinary process to be applied in cases of abuse.

Management should be at the forefront and lead by example but this wasn't always how it happened...

Foreigners
In days gone by it was common to see 'foreigners' (e.g. fixing the sales director's outboard motor for his boat) being done in company time out on the shopfloor. A colleague once spent an entire day combing local builders merchants and reclamation yards trying to match a brick given him by one of the directors.

To build a new factory?

No, to enable the director to erect a small shelter outside his front door as a shady spot for his milk delivery.

IT
A particular director sat at his desk staring at his IT manager's expenditure request. Following complaints about slow-computer speeds, the manager wanted to spend a substantial amount of money upgrading internet links. But the director had his doubts

and launched an investigation. The IT department was asked to monitor internet use and it was established that not only were a significant number of employees accessing websites for personal use on a regular basis throughout their working day, but some were even coming in on paid overtime to carry out tasks such as paying bills. Believing that lax management had played a significant role in this state of affairs, rather than immediately initiating disciplinary action against the worst culprits, the director explained to the workforce why the current situation was untenable. Clear instructions were given detailing the circumstances under which the business would allow IT equipment to be used for personal rather than business purposes. The consequences, in disciplinary terms, for non-compliance were also made clear.

Aware of company policy, and that the information was available and would be used to confront those abusing the rules, internet usage fell by 50%, computer speeds for both internet use and internal transactions increased dramatically... and the director ripped up the expenditure request.

In practice

- Make sure there is clear policy that is consistently applied on appropriate uses of company time, and that disciplinary action is taken on an even-handed basis.

- It is important to lead by example in setting company culture. Management may be seen to be the worst offenders. Step back and consider how your behaviours may influence others.

- 'Brown bag' meetings at the start of the day are not a replacement for a clearly defined and implemented policy on attendance... but may provide a useful reminder of when thoughts should turn to business rather than personal matters.

STARING INTO SPACE

SPACE COSTS MONEY.

If you own it you've got capital locked up in it that is costing you interest. If you don't own it you've got rent to pay.

In either case you have rates, maintenance costs, heating bills...

But that's not all.

What about the opportunity cost? What else could you do with some freed-up space?

The idea

Think creatively about floorspace.

Don't just accept the 'We've got 5 years left on the lease so we can't down-size until then' argument.

If you're stuck with existing floorspace costs, take the opportunity to do more with it... any space you can free is effectively exactly that, free!

Get organised!
How often do you hear people wish that they could 'start again' on a greenfield site so that they organise their processes such that products flowed better through the business? If only there were some free space...

Are people working in a muddle because there isn't space to organise workspaces properly? If only there were some free space...

This company was reluctant to accept that there was a great reason to organise floorspace more efficiently. They seemed to have completely forgotten about the £20,000 per annum in rent they were paying for a unit at a trading estate a few miles away, in which they were storing redundant tooling. By reorganising layouts, they were able to accommodate the stores on-site (and at the same time were encouraged to re-think which tooling really had to be kept).

Find a partner!
This coffee-shop re-organised its seating so that a local newspaper retailer could rent vending space.

Another manufacturer used surplus space on the shopfloor to sub-let to a supplier who could then move his products directly on to the manufacturing line as and when required.

Flaunt it!
And if you've no immediate use for the space, report on it separately as an 'enabler' (see IDEA 50) to highlight the opportunity on offer.

By ruthlessly clearing unnecessary occupied floorspace and cordoning off the resulting vacated area of the factory, this other manufacturing unit was excellently placed for winning the contract to build the new product.

In practice

- Motivate people to use floorspace efficiently by charging out a cost for space as part of departmental expenses.

- When any floorspace is released, remove the charge for it from departmental spend and report on it separately as the cost of unutilised space to focus everyone's attention on possible profitable uses.

64 STARS, COWS AND DOGS

WHERE YOUR PRODUCTS or services are on the life-cycle will influence their cost. Knowing what stage they are in can also help direct you towards particularly relevant cost-improvement ideas.

The idea

Manage your product costs with reference to their stage on the life-cycle.

The life-cycle of demand for products and services can come in all shapes and sizes but is usually similar to the one shown below:

DIAGRAM 1

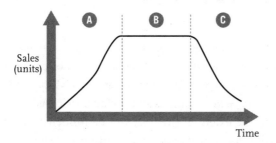

The 'A' stage can be referred to as the 'star' stage and covers product or service launch and the subsequent period of relatively rapid sales growth up until the point where sales volumes are beginning to level out.

As sales volumes stabilise, the product or service enters the 'B' stage. This is known as the 'cow' stage (often called the 'cash-cow' stage as the business seeks to 'milk' as much cash out of the product as they can).

Fashions change and technology moves on. When sales volume starts to drop off the 'C' stage starts – often called the 'sea-dog' stage because too many dogs (i.e. too much complexity) and you drown. You have to know when to start cutting the dogs' tails off.

Consider what is happening to the cost of your product or service. Again, each product or service will have its own variant but in most instances, as volumes increase and you iron out those teething problems, you expect costs to fall.

DIAGRAM 2

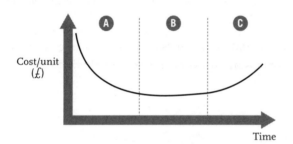

Of course how fast and how long your costs continue to fall depends on whether you've managed to inculcate a culture of continuous improvement where everyone is out hunting the next opportunity to do more with less. When volumes start to fall back costs may rise – but once again the extent of this rise will be influenced by how you respond to this down-turn in demand. Setting aside the issue of lemmings (see below), are you able to re-think your process to find a more cost-effective method appropriate for the changed pattern of demand (see IDEA 47)?

(Take another look at that cost curve. Is this what your costing system tells you? Don't believe everything you read! Before you use your costing system for decision-making check out IDEA 26.)

Don't forget that the amount of cash flowing into or out of the business will also affect your business costs as it will determine how much you have to borrow, and hence the cost of interest payments on that borrowed money.

During the 'A' stage, cash is pouring out of the business as you invest in the facilities and processes you need, lay down stock and wait to collect money from the customer. Which is why you need some products or services to be in the next stage.

As it says on the label, the 'B' stage, or cash-cow stage is when, if you get it right, cash should pour back into the business as you earn decent margins on your products and your investment falls (see IDEA 52).

Did you pick up on when you enter the 'C' stage? Those who fail to notice the 'edge-of-the-cliff' at the end of the B stage of the demand curve, like lemmings, keep on going when there is no demand (or ground) to support them. 'Lemmings' will eventually notice increasing stock levels (and the consequential outflow of cash) as failing to read the market leads to being late in 'turning off the tap'. Otherwise, continuous careful re-alignment of how you do things to reflect what the market wants should allow you to continue to generate cash in the 'dog' stage. If you can't – and you're not contractually obliged to continue to supply – cut off that tail!

In practice

- Identify where your products or services are on the demand life-cycle to gain an insight into the associated financial threats and opportunities.

- If you're looking for ideas for the 'star' stage try IDEAS 32, 76 & 97.

- For the 'cow' stage look at the hazards discussed in IDEAS 52 & 89.

- Avoid drowning in the 'dog' stage by looking at IDEAS 47 & 61.

STORING UP TROUBLE

Some people just can't throw things away. Yet de-cluttering workspaces can have a therapeutic effect and allow people to work more efficiently (see IDEA 42). The same goes for information.

The idea

Just as you need to review how much slow-moving and obsolete inventory you hold (see IDEA 75), you also need to think about the information you hold.

What do you keep in your archives?

Industrial archaeology

Sometimes you have to be ruthless with hoarders. This new office manager was intrigued by the expanse of filing cabinets surrounding one of the long-service employees in the office. He subsequently found out that these cabinets contained a copy of every memo the employee had received or sent out in his 35 years working for the business. While an archivist might have been interested in the Christmas lunch arrangements of another era...

Others create chaos by not keeping appropriate records. (Although you might recall instances in politics when inadvertent shredding of documents that should have been preserved has proved fortuitous...)

Think space doesn't matter? If you're talking about physical documents and physical space, IDEAS 54 & 63 can give you some examples of how that space could be used.

If you're talking about computer files and storage, just ask your IT manager about the benefits to be had from freeing up space.

In the doc

Unable to face the grim process of submitting yet another request for capital expenditure, this time for additional file storage, the IT manager in this organisation decided to take a closer look at what exactly people were storing. Delving deep into archived information, he found substantial files with all the technical and commercial information (including pictures) for every contract the company had ever won. Twice. Continuing his preparations for spring-cleaning, he found more and more instances of replicated information held not only by different departments but even by different individuals in the same department.

It was time to issue custodial sentences. Each category of information is now 'owned' by a specific department who are responsible for holding it in their files. Access is clearly defined with protocols of who can amend the information and those who can access on a read-only basis.

(Not only has this saved on file storage but it has also provided a common database with all additions or amendments to the information being centralised in one location.)

In practice

- Identify legal and commercial requirements for storing information and then implement a procedure defining who keeps what, where it is kept, who is responsible for maintaining the record and the access protocols.

- Make an explanation of this procedure an integral part of any new employee's induction process.

66 STRAIGHT TO THE BOTTOM LINE!

CHECK YOUR COMPLETED orders.

If there's work you've done that hasn't been invoiced then get on and do it – you've incurred the cost, now claim your reward (see IDEA 32)! Have you invoiced everything you're entitled to?

Did you invoice at the correct price? Unsurprisingly, customers rarely complain when they are under-charged – is everyone working from the right price list (see IDEA 14)?

What about expenses such as postage and packaging (see IDEA 93)?

Is it time to increase your prices?

The idea

If you can increase your price without reducing the amount you sell, then the increase goes straight to the bottom line. And the ability to increase your prices might be already written into some of your contracts.

Do any of your contracts with your customers have escalation clauses? Have you considered using them in your quotations?

Escalation clauses allow for timely re-negotiations on price with customers with claims for price-increases substantiated by the movement in relevant costs indices to the business. This can take some of the heat out of discussions. Look at the type of costs you incur and where your greatest risk-exposures are and make sure those negotiating on your behalf get the best deal they can. It's worth noting that escalation clauses rarely cover all aspects of the price – with say 20% of the price not subject to escalation, 40% escalated on the agreed material index and 40% on the agreed labour index. To maintain your margins you therefore have to improve your performance to more than out-strip the inflationary pressures on whatever fixed element has been agreed. There are plenty of ideas in this book to start you off!

For escalation clauses to work effectively, indices must be clearly specified and should track the cost movements you are experiencing as closely as possible. Choose material indices that reflect cost movements in the materials you are using – an index tracking generalised metal prices will not match the cost increases you're facing on any specific metal. Record the agreed baseline. Monitor movements in the relevant indices on a regular basis – and make sure the indices have not been discontinued. Should this happen, contact your customer immediately and agree an alternative methodology.

And most importantly of all... don't forget to trigger any increases!

Rising excitement

A team of anxious senior managers sat staring at the figures in front of them. Locked into a 10 year contract with a further 5 years to run and rocked by spiralling metal prices, they were already making losses and, despite their best efforts, with little realistic hope of further significant cost-improvement the situation looked bleak. With sighs all round they decided it would be worth combing through the contract in hope of finding a get-out clause. They didn't. But what they did find was far more valuable.

Years ago a shrewd commercial negotiator (who had since left the business) had agreed on escalation clauses that had never been triggered. And this wasn't the only contract where the opportunity to make something for nothing had been missed.

Now there is a visual display of all current contracts on the wall in the commercial department, colour-coded to denote the nature of any escalation clauses negotiated and the timing of the next trigger-points.

In practice

- Don't miss your opportunity to make something for nothing!

- Check on existing contract conditions.

- Make sure you're charging customers for everything you're entitled to invoice for – and at the correct price.

- Determine contract risk – and then manage it by negotiating escalation clauses.

TAKEN TO THE CLEANERS

Why is it that buying products is considered less angst-ridden than buying services?

When you are purchasing tangible objects, you can check them against the specification on the order and inspect them for quality. You know how many you ordered and when delivery was due.

So what's different about service contracts?

The idea

You're asking for trouble with service contracts if you haven't a formal agreement detailing the specification of the services to be carried out, the standard of performance expected, and the frequency with which the service is to be performed.

Couple any lack of clarity with the service being performed at a time when there is little customer visibility, usually little service-provider supervision and often inadequate measures of performance and what do you have...

Cleaning contracts.

We all know what we mean by cleaning – don't we? (Anyone with teenage children will understand the vastly differing interpretations that can be applied to this word.)

Just as you wouldn't go into a hairdressers and give them carte blanche to do whatever they wanted to do to your hair while you took a short nap (unless you are very trusting or phenomenally disinterested in your appearance), neither can you assume that your service provider can read your mind and share your standards.

A new broom

Having heard of the constant problems this business had suffered with cleaners over many years, this newly-appointed facilities manager adopted a fresh approach. The process of negotiating contracts now starts by issuing a standardised template to the manager of each discrete area of the buildings, listing the possible cleaning activities required. Each manager completes the template indicating not only which activities are required, but also the amount of work entailed (e.g. number of windows to clean) and the frequency with which the service is required. Where a standard of cleaning is non-negotiable (e.g. clean rooms) this is also recorded.

This information is then summarised with the performance measures to be used and 'Gold, Silver and Bronze' standards clearly defined. This document is then put out to quote. (It is important to ask service providers to quote for alternative standards of performance so you can take an informed decision about best value-for-money.)

This may initially seem hard work. However, once you have a clear understanding of the service to be performed, you can then set about eliminating unnecessary activities just as you would with activities undertaken by your own workforce. For instance, centralising recycling facilities in offices, rather than allowing everyone their own bin, not only reduces garbage collection costs but also the cleaning activity required. This puts you in a great position when it comes to mid-term or annual contract reviews.

Seek tenders on a regular basis. Contract creep is insidious.

Monitor and review

When monitoring performance it's useful to have sign-offs for areas such as toilets. While in itself it doesn't guarantee the work is properly done, having a name put to it does increase the probability... but effective supervision is better still!

To ensure there are regular reviews and that the selected supplier focuses on delivering what they have promised, this one business negotiates to retain 25% of the management fee until the supplier has met at least 90% of their targets.

In practice

- List your service providers and dig out the contracts.

- Check that you been crystal clear about what is expected and the measurements to be taken to monitor whether performance is to the agreed standard.

TAKING STOCK

You MAY HAVE been reading about the benefits of reducing the amount of money you have tied up in stock and even some of the great ideas about how to go about this.

However, one not-so-great idea is for the stock to just disappear without trace. What is sometimes referred to as 'shrinkage' is really theft.

The idea

Every bit of stock-loss is a cost to the business. Would you leave bundles of £50 notes lying around the yard or in a consumable or stationery store with everyone free to help themselves?

Unfortunately, not all employees discriminate between what belongs to the company and what belongs to them. Lax management control can breed a culture where what might be considered 'petty theft' is considered a perk of the job.

Caught on camera
A film crew wished to shoot a scene showing a large workforce pouring out of a factory. Managers of this automotive company agreed to keep the gates temporarily shut at the end of a shift. Once sufficient numbers of people had built up waiting to leave, the gates would be opened and the film shot taken. The workforce however, unaware of what was going on, concluded people were being searched as they left the premises. When all those on the shift had left, the managers were amazed by the parts, assemblies and consumables littering the yard.

Forking out
Another organisation noticed seasonal variation in their spend

on canteen equipment... as the camping and caravanning season started, cutlery would start to disappear from the dining hall.

Extra to boot

Protective footwear was provided by this company as part of delivering a safe working environment on the shopfloor. To maintain adequate protection, replacement shoes were issued from stores on an annual basis. Noticing the rather poor condition of footwear of a number of employees, the manager decided to check the records for issuing new boots. She was astonished to find that while new boots were being regularly issued, some individuals' shoe sizes appeared to alter very dramatically from one year to another. On investigation it was found that the new boots were being passed to friends, other family members... or appeared at the local car boot sale.

And while we're on the subject of car-boot sales, that's exactly where this surprised manager found one of his company's rather large aerospace components for sale (see IDEA 58).

In practice

- Make sure the management team has a clear and consistent understanding of what constitutes 'theft' from the business and the consequences of such action.

- Communicate this to everyone in the workforce, then put in highly visible controls on a couple of key items to signal that you are serious about this.

- Identify those items most likely to walk and make sure they are being properly managed.

- Remember that every cost incurred by the business should have a customer willing to pay for it – not an employee willing to take it.

TARGETING RESOURCES

WHAT PLANS DO you have for the business next year?

Most people have a pretty clear picture of what their plans are – but ask them to set a budget and they go weak at the knees. If you have a well-thought-out plan you've done the difficult part. All a budget does is attach £ notes to that plan.

You need to do a budget because you need to make sure the plan stacks up in terms of meeting your financial objectives.

How much profit do you need to make? Or want to make?

Will you be able to generate enough cash to keep the business turning while it earns that profit?

Once you have that financial plan you're in a much better situation to control, monitor and improve those costs (see IDEA 35).

So where do you start?

Try working top-down then bottom-up.

The idea

If the plan's going to make sense it has to be co-ordinated. There is no point in the manufacturing manager planning to invest in additional machines to increase capacity by 50% if the sales forecast shows a decline in business. So start with the big picture and the limiting factor – i.e. the aspect of the plan that forms the constraint. In most businesses this is the volume of sales they believe they can achieve, but it could be for instance the availability of a particular raw material or specialist labour skills. Once you've done this you can use it as the framework to breakdown responsibilities for each part of the plan, and then build up the costs that will have to be incurred to achieve it.

If you are a departmental manager or other budget-holder, start your involvement with the budgeting process by asking a question. "What do you need me to do next year?" Only when you know what is expected of you (and the timeframe in which it has to be achieved) can you decide how you're going to go about delivering that responsibility, the resources you will therefore need, and only then, last of all, comes the step of attaching financial costs to those resources.

What if it doesn't add up?

Sadly, the reality is that when all the costs are totted up the plan is often financially unsustainable, so budgets have to be re-worked on an iterative approach – either by fundamentally re-thinking the constraint, or changing the way activities are organised to deliver the plan, or finding realistic ways of accessing cheaper resources until an acceptable budget is reached.

Rather than use this iterative approach (or the less rational application of an axe to budgets), some organisations report back to budget-holders the extent of the 'strive' – the savings necessary to achieve an acceptable plan. There is then a collective responsibility to work together to effect savings to achieve this strive.

In practice

- Understand the threats and opportunities to achieving your plan – protracted winter weather-conditions will have very different financial impacts for the supplier of road salt from the council having to organise its use.

- While information about past expenditure can help with budget-setting, make sure you adjust for any exceptional spends (see IDEA 19) and recognise the differences between the plan and what has gone before.

- Beware of those who brag about size. Judge people not by the size of their budgets, but how effectively they use every £ they spend to achieve their part of the team plan.

70 TBA – TO BE AVOIDED

In the chase for additional business, salespeople can occasionally overlook minor details – such as agreeing how much the customer is going to pay.

(If so, what is the likelihood that they'll also remember to negotiate other critical details, such as *when* the customer is going to pay!)

The idea

While no doubt most of your customers are honourable people, this is not a position in which you want to put yourself. TBAs (orders with prices To Be Agreed) should not be an acceptable basis for authorising work to commence as it leaves you vulnerable to having taken on loss-making work (without this being a conscious decision) or, at worst, with no recovery of your costs at all.

You can get caught at an unguarded moment. A valued customer (or one you'd love to get on your books) calls you frantic for help. They need you to make a rush order (or drop everything to carry out a service) to get them out of a fix. With the comment, "Don't worry we'll sort out the paperwork later," they're gone.

Disaster in the making

This disaster-recovery business fell victim to a TBA and needed a little help themselves. A prestigious organisation, about to open a landmark facility, was making arrangements for the forthcoming opening ceremony when it started to rain. Through the roof of the VIP box. In the ensuing panic the disaster-recovery business was contacted and employees, contractors and materials were rushed to the site. Working against the clock, temporary repairs were carried out and by the time the scissors were raised to cut the ribbon, it was sunny smiles all round. The recovery team even returned after the ceremony for another couple of days' work to carry out a permanent fix. The organisation was delighted with the service they had received and the quality of the work carried out and were generous in their offers to recommend the company to others.

They were not so generous, however, in paying the bill!

Apparently unable to pay until they had recovered the cost from their insurers, the recovery business was told it would have to wait. With no contractual payment terms in place there was little they could do but bide their time and learn their lesson.

And the boot can be on the other foot.

It can be very easy when under pressure to rush to find a solution to a predicament without waiting long enough to negotiate and agree terms. If the machine has broken down and you can't get the customer's order out...

You could end up with a bill you'd never bargained for!

In practice

- Insist on the customer placing an order before you start work – in an emergency it can be faxed over to you or given to you on your arrival at the site. Don't forget to check those terms and conditions!

- If you are in a business where the nature of the work makes it difficult to set a final price, agree on the core price (preferably with formalised stage payments) and the basis (and timescale) on which 'extras' are to be agreed, invoiced... and paid!

71 TELL PEOPLE WHAT THINGS COST

WITH REFERENCE TO stationery and other consumables, you often hear the complaint that people wouldn't waste so much 'if it was their own money'. Perhaps one of the reasons behind the waste is lack of information rather than just a question of who's footing the bill.

The idea

If you want people to be cost-conscious, they have to be conscious of cost!

Handy information

A newly appointed manufacturing manager was concerned about the high level of spend on protective gloves. When he explained to his team how much each pair of gloves cost they were horrified. The result? Not only did gloves get treated as consumable rather than disposable items, the buyer also shopped around and sourced an alternative glove that met requirements, lasted just as long and was much cheaper.

Emergency action

A delegate on a course recommended using an old style pricing gun to put a price tag on all items in stores, stationery cupboards, consumable stations etc. He did this in an A&E unit in Waterford and, without taking any other action, saw the consumable costs come down by 15%. Apparently his greatest problem was admitting the simplicity of his idea to the Hospital Management Team!

The price is – what?

Run on similar lines to popular gameshows, as the 'warm-up' at the start of a briefing session, another company asked employees to match costs to pictures of consumable items. Interestingly, even after being given the individual prices, many were unable to rank the items by annual total spend.

In practice

* Get hold of a pricing gun!

* To grab attention and encourage people to think twice, put up visually attractive cost information at the point of use. This may have the double win of not only reducing immediate usage, but also triggering bright ideas of how to re-engineer the task to avoid using the item at all.

  (And while on the subject of usage – a centralised stationery cupboard with items signed out to individuals has been known to work wonders!)

72 THAT'S WHAT YOU ORDERED

It's really important to be specific about what you need from your suppliers.

Every £1 you spend on products or services that aren't exactly what you need keeps that shredder busy (see IDEA 90).

The idea

If suppliers are to get it right, you need to be clear on what you need and you have to communicate this properly.

A company bought in precision-made components from a supplier with an excellent record for quality. Inspected against the drawings, these small components passed first time every time. But the company was having a problem with a high reject-rate on the assemblies into which these components went. Eventually it emerged that while the components agreed to the drawings supplied, these drawings were insufficiently detailed with regard to what subsequently emerged as critical tolerances and finishes on an internal bore. For commercial reasons it would be prohibitively expensive to change the drawings. The solution? The component was brought back in-house and a method developed for creating the bore that would deliver the tolerance and finish required.

The moral of the story?

There is actually more than one. Besides providing a reminder of how important it is to know exactly what it is you want and to communicate this clearly to your suppliers, it's an excellent example of where small may be beautiful – but can certainly be expensive. These components were small so it was assumed they were cheap. Before the problem had been highlighted, whenever the assembly failed test, the component would be removed, thrown in the bin and another one tried until eventually the unit passed.

Had the assembly-worker known that the component cost £44 a time, action to address the problem would hopefully have been taken sooner.

In practice

- If you bring goods into the business that aren't exactly what you need, you're going to end up incurring unnecessary cost so it pays to be precise.

- Buyers are not psychic! Make sure your design team works closely with manufacturing to ascertain precisely what is required and that this is communicated clearly to those in purchasing.

THE DEATH SPIRAL

Be careful when preparing information to be used for cost comparisons with other manufacturing sites.

If you use absorption costing to do this, it could lead to wrong assumptions about what products cost to make in different locations, and drive sub-optimal choices as to where to manufacture both existing and new products.

The idea

Once on the spiral of decline, if you don't present information appropriately, it's difficult to escape.

Spiralling costs
This engineering business made a range of aerospace products with sizeable capacity for a new product about to be launched. Technical problems with other aspects of the aircraft caused their customer to suspend the schedule until these issues were resolved. Unable to slash their business costs in response, according to the costing system, the cost of the other products the manufacturer made increased as the system forced them to absorb the costs of the unused capacity.

Concerned about the spiralling costs of their ongoing business, work was shipped out to other sites and 'low cost economies' so that the apparent costs of the work remaining on the site rose even higher so...

Of course, the spiral can also work the other way.

Spiralling success

A dynamic manufacturing unit of a global producer had the opportunity to take on additional work at little more than material costs because, through improvement activities, they had freed-up the necessary capacity and floorspace. The absorption costing system passed the benefit of being able to spread business costs over a larger volume of products on to all its existing products, so with lower product costs more work was loaded on to the site so product costs fell away further...

In practice

- Be extremely wary of the uses to which you put your costing system.

- Segregate the cost of unutilised capacity and report on it separately. This will prevent distorting cost information for other products and focus management attention on either filling this capacity with profitable work, or scaling down the business in line with market needs.

THE SMELL OF MONEY

When dealing with worrisome by-products or dangerous substances, in your concern for people's health and the impact on the environment, you can be taken for an expensive ride.

The idea

If you're out of your depth or sinking in the mire, get advice from a reliable source.

Some by-products are relatively straight-forward.

Water
Your water company probably assumes that what goes in must come out and charges accordingly. If you have alternative arrangements for collecting water from roofs or hard surfaces or you're not connected to mains sewerage, make sure you're not paying more than you should.

Oils and solvents
It costs you to dispose of oils and solvents properly. Do you recover these costs wherever possible? Simple filtering can be effective and most solvents can be distilled. For example, when tramp oil (the lubricant for machining centres) gets mixed with coolant it can be separated, filtered then re-used.

So what do you do when you have a problem that you don't fully comprehend? You take advice from the experts, don't you?

Dramatic events
Despite specific warnings, a firm of local builders replacing panels on the outside of this factory used welding equipment without

permission and set fire to a section of the roof. The roof comprised several layers of different materials, including one of low-grade asbestos. The buildings were evacuated, the fire brigade arrived and so did a representative of the Environment Agency.

Given the presence of asbestos, the company was told to call in contractors who specialised in removing asbestos for advice. They did so and were told that testing showed that there was a higher than acceptable level of asbestos present in the factory. The firm prescribed the quarantining of all production areas – not just in the factory building in which the fire had started, but also in all adjacent buildings. The company, concerned for their employees' health and anxious to get the factory up and running again as soon as possible, approved the plan.

Looking more like a film-set for a disaster movie, the area became infested with white-suited people as zones were partitioned off with plastic screens and the clean-up started. Equipment that couldn't be easily 'de-contaminated' (such as computers) were bagged up and taken to specialist landfill sites.

A few days later, the managers became uneasy that what had been a fairly minor incident had been escalated out of all proportion. Contacting the Factory Inspector, they asked for his advice. (Many people regard the Factory Inspector as a close relative to the Tax Inspector to be kept at arms length whenever possible. But he does have a wealth of experience – or access to those who have – of dealing with all sorts of factory incidents and can offer that steadying hand in situations where things might seem to have got out of control.)

Having spoken to colleagues and contacts in other businesses that had experienced similar events, the view was that the actions being taken did appear somewhat extreme. It was considered unlikely that a localised fire would have impacted such a widespread area and the managers were advised to call in a team of experts from a different organisation (with no vested interest in the subsequent clean-up operation), to carry out tests in each area of each building. Their tests revealed that there was only a small area of one factory (about 10 sq m) where there was contamination. This 'coincidentally' had been the area the original contractors had selected to test to vindicate their recommendation for a site-wide operation.

The manager recounting this tale felt that the moral of the story was that when a hopefully once-in-a-lifetime incident such as this occurs, you are very vulnerable and will clutch the first life-raft that comes your way. Don't get rescued by pirates. Use your contacts and get a second opinion (see IDEA 33).

In practice

- Check the removal costs of all your waste products.

- Explore ways to recycle and save money (see IDEA 11).

- Find other organisations that could use your waste – there are plenty of agencies out there ready to act as marriage brokers.

- Build a network of expert knowledge that you can trust (see IDEA 33).

75 TO KEEP OR NOT TO KEEP

You have inventory on the shelf. It just might come in useful sometime. You've already written it off so... do you keep it? It isn't costing you anything – is it?

Yes, it is.

Perhaps it has a scrap value and you could turn it into valuable cash?

If you hang on to it you're also forgoing the opportunity to do something better with the floorspace (IDEA 63), to clear the decks of distractions and to save the administrative cost of all that record keeping (IDEA 54)... unless you're secretly hoping it will disappear of its own accord (IDEA 68).

If you're concerned about disposal costs, try being creative and finding someone who would be delighted to take it off your hands (see IDEA 11).

The idea

In some instances, 'hoarding' can pay off – especially if you're selective about what you hoard...

We all know about the impact of the rapid rate of change in technology in the electronic components industry. This company supplied a product stuffed full of electronic components for the Concorde. With a limited number of the aircraft still flying, the business, no longer contractually obliged to provide spares, received an order for a product full of obsolete electronic components. Reminding the customer that there were no longer any sources of supply for the components that went into the product, the shrewd supplier said they did just happen to have one complete unit in inventory... There was nowhere else the customer could go. To change the specification of the part would require phenomenal amounts of time and money on the requisite testing and re-qualification.

With no on-going relationship with the customer to maintain, the supplier was in a position to charge a price that rewarded them not just for the costs tied up in keeping that unit in inventory for all that time, but probably the total warehousing costs they had incurred for many years!

In practice

- Take a cold hard look at everything you keep on a 'just-in-case' basis.

- Even inventory that has been written-off is costing you money – decide where there are commercial reasons for gambling that this investment will eventually pay off and where you would be better off releasing the cost and being occasionally caught-out with the costs of fulfilling a 'one-off' order (see IDEA 61).

76 TOO SUCCESSFUL TO SURVIVE!

WILL BREAKING INTO the big time finish you off?

The salesman races in clutching the order and the celebrations begin. You've just won a huge order on which you're predicted to make a great margin... what could possibly go wrong?

Let's assume the product or service is clearly defined, your costing system is reasonable, your supply chain is 100% reliable, your workforce excellent, your processes world-class and you're confident that if you start now you can make the first delivery on time three months from now.

Have you forgotten anything?

Who is going to finance this additional business?

The idea

Growing the business can be a precarious matter, so you need to plan cashflows carefully.

You're going to have to start forking out for materials, payroll costs, expenses (and possibly new equipment) months before the first shipment... and even when that has been invoiced, how much credit has the over-eager salesman been prepared to offer his customer?

How much money are you going to have to borrow to see this through and, if you can last that long, by then how much of your 'great margin' will have been eaten away by interest costs?

Can you afford to change your business model?

Food for thought

A wholesaler selling food into small retail outlets decided to move into the big time and develop his own brand of ready-meals. The change from running a business where products were turned over very rapidly and sold for cash to one requiring substantial investment and customers who demanded credit was too much and the business folded.

A complete lack of understanding and control of costs doesn't help either!

Blinded by hope

This business was brought to the brink of failure having been lured by the opportunity of a substantial amount of new business. Winning the order would require the business to self-fund the product development, but would then allow them exclusive access to high volumes of profitable work.

Quoting for business arguably out of their league, and short of resources, the team preparing the quotation drew on their salesman for help. A salesman who was desperate to win the business. A salesman who was renowned for his eternal optimism. The initial estimate of the cost of the development work was £3m. So, being prudent, they doubled it and prepared their quote on the assumption that their up-front outlay could rise to £6m. Unfortunately, they won the contract. Had it not been for a timely acquisition by another business, the eventual development costs of £60m would have buried them.

In practice

* When quoting for new business, make sure you keep your eye firmly on whether you can afford to take the order rather than being fixated by the prospect of future profits.

- Work through the impact on Working Capital and consider ways to manage the additional investment by, for example, purchasing goods from suppliers on credit, speeding up the lead time through the business, negotiating progress payments and balancing the trade-off between price and customer credit.

- Orders for new products or services are inherently more risky, so just make sure that when you take them on you're not signing your own death warrant.

TRAINED TO PERFECTION

You've got a great team – but do they have the necessary skills to realise their potential and bring maximum value to the business?

The idea

If you ask what is a business' most valuable resource, you'll usually be told it's their people. It can also be their most expensive.

Take a look at how much you spend on payroll costs and make sure your team is achieving their potential.

It's not what you do...
Training for specific tasks is not just about what needs to be achieved but also the manner or method in which it is done.

IDEA 46 looked at the potential cost improvements in reduced scrap and warranty work by reducing variability in the manufacturing process and the advantages of using workplace expertise to determine the best way to standardise methods. Teams tend to enjoy videoing each other doing the task and then deciding for themselves the standardised method to be adopted. With this approach, not only do operatives take ownership of the method but it also facilitates skills transfer with videos and visual instructions for subsequent training purposes.

IDEA 21 considered the potential additional income that can be generated by having a personable, well-trained team out on the restaurant floor.

Achilles' heels

Try to avoid single-point failure (where there is a critical operation for which only one person has the required knowledge or expertise) by cross-training to develop a flexible workforce (see IDEA 60).

Win-wins

In your team there will be those considered for future promotion. Their personal development needs may extend beyond the acquisition of specific skills and be of a more generalised nature. Some businesses, trying to juggle their training budgets, have hit upon a great solution by offering employee time to charitable organisations for specific projects. The employee and project are matched appropriately; the employee gains from the experience, the charity gains from an expert free pair of hands – and the business wins again with the opportunity to promote their commitment to the wider community.

Flexibility

Do some team members require regular re-accreditation of knowledge and skills to be appropriately qualified for the work they are doing?

Re-accreditation of skills is a necessary but potentially time-consuming and hence costly process. A physiotherapist recounted how the situation in her authority had been much improved by using e-learning where appropriate.

Physiotherapists in this particular health authority are required to undergo regular re-accreditation for a wide variety of work-related issues from infection control through safeguarding to fire training. Annual half-day training sessions would be booked to cover a range of topics necessitating clearing diaries of clinical work for a number of staff who would all be away from the department and the wards at the same time. Almost invariably, one of the appointed trainers would be called away on an emergency, resulting in wasted time and the need to reconvene the group at a later date with a further negative effect on clinical availability.

Training requirements are now monitored automatically and delivered through e-learning wherever appropriate, giving physios control over their learning and accreditation. With access to their own training records, physios are advised when re-accreditation needs to take place and have certification to provide evidence of successful completion. The e-learning has been structured in such a way that physios can complete parts of modules as and when they have time available (either planned or unplanned), allowing them to ensure they have the requisite up-to-date skills while minimising the disruption to their clinical responsibilities.

In practice

- Just as you would look to maintain and upgrade your equipment, pay similar attention to your staff.

- Check out the surprising amount of 'free' training available out there that you've already paid for through your taxes!

TROUBLE IN STORES

WHAT IS YOUR business going to do for itself and what is it going to pay someone else to do?

IDEA 89 looks at the challenges of using information from your costing system to determine 'make-buy' decisions on manufacturing matters, but what about those other activities you carry out?

There are strategic issues to consider first such as:

- Would you be outsourcing a key success criterion and/or help nurture a competitor?

- Would the business become vulnerable should the supplier fail – or change allegiance?

- Would outsourcing create problems of confidentiality?

Once you've sorted those strategic matters and you're still up for outsourcing, you need to consider the financial implications.

The idea

When evaluating outsourcing decisions, look at the incrementals. List and value the extra costs you will incur, and weigh them against the savings you will make.

Kitted out

Take the example of a business deciding to purchase complete kits rather than multiple individual items from which they used to marshall kits themselves. Although they may have to pay the selected supplier a management fee for doing this, the opportunities for cost improvement are there.

With no kit marshalling on site, space is released, and activities in purchasing, receiving, stores, production scheduling and administration are subsequently reduced. With less money tied up in inventory, there are interest savings to be made.

All this sounds great... but how much money is actually saved?

You may be told that it costs your business say £80 to raise a purchase order. But if buying kits rather than parts saves you raising as many purchase orders, will £80 of cost disappear for every purchase order you eliminate?

Be brutal. Be realistic.

While arguably by outsourcing you create spare capacity even in a non-manufacturing process, this 'cost saving' has a sneaky habit of evaporating before your very eyes.

If a proposal is purported to 'remove the work of two people' it doesn't actually save you anything until you either reduce the payroll costs (through natural wastage or redundancy), or use the time released to do other 'value creating' work – i.e. activities that customers will pay for.

Away from the measuring mentality of the production shop, there is a tendency to find 'useful' (as opposed to 'value creating') work in perpetuity.

And outsourcing can have some unintended consequences.

Savings – what savings?
This business had its own toolstores run by employed storekeepers. As part of the drive to improve costs (and which by a happy coincidence also improved the 'headcount' figure reported to head office) it was decided to outsource the stores allowing a supplier to effectively run a rent-free 'shop' on their premises.

So far so good.

Not only were there savings in workload in purchasing, receiving and stores (leading eventually to either savings in payroll costs or the opportunity to divert those hours to 'value creating' work), the business also no longer had their own money tied up in tools on the shelf.

Even better.

What had been overlooked was the need to implement more stringent controls on the number and type of tools being issued. It was in the interest of the 'shop' to encourage people to use more new and expensive tools with the result that spend increased dramatically. Only when this had been sorted did the business see an overall improvement in cost.

In practice

- Look for opportunities to focus on the activities that are core to your business and at which you excel, and consider the case for outsourcing others.

- Be realistic, however, on the savings you will make by outsourcing. The better you liaise with your selected supplier to smooth out all the 'rough edges' in the way the service is provided, the more you'll save. If you get it right, the only place you'll notice the change is on your bottom line. If you get it wrong...

79 UNDER PRESSURE

ARE YOU LEAKING money?

When everything stops out in the factory can you hear the hiss of wasted money?

A hole the size of a match head in a compressed air pipeline can waste enough energy in a working day to make 444 slices of toast.

That's a lot of bread.

The idea

Most factories cannot operate without compressed air. Because of this, the emphasis tends to be on the reliability of supply rather than issues of efficiency and hence cost effectiveness. But compressors that are reliable and need minimal maintenance could still be costing you a small fortune.

Compressors can be hugely inefficient – up to 95% of the electrical energy consumed may be lost as heat with only around 5% being used to compress air. A compressor running a single shift in a year can cost as much in electricity as its entire capital cost.

So this utility is very expensive but doesn't attract the attention it so richly deserves. When you consider that using compressed air can cost you almost 10 times the cost of using electricity, it changes your mindset. Only use compressed air when you have no other options and use the lowest pressure you can. Use variable speed compressors so that you only produce what you need when you need it. Think about where you should locate your compressors. Old factories often have them miles away from the point of use leading to pressure drops and increased likelihood of leaks. If you have machines or processes that require increased pressures (or special qualities such as oil-free air), it might pay to have a localised compressor rather than 'over-engineering' the air supplied elsewhere. Local portable machines might be the sensible solution if you have a few machines running over the weekend.

Gasping for air

A well-known manufacturer of breakfast cereals was proud of its maintenance team who like Scotty on the Enterprise could keep equipment running forever. While the compressor manufacturers recommended that key components were changed after 36,000 hours of use, these wizards had kept the compressors going for 90,000 hours. They thought they were saving their employer money. What they didn't consider was the impact of their ingenuity on the electricity bill that was hidden away as a day-to-day operational expense. When they finally accepted defeat and invested in new energy-efficient compressors electricity usage dropped. By 50%.

In practice

- Measure the cost of energy used to run your compressors.

- Carry out an audit of your demands for compressed air.

- Get advice on more cost-effective solutions – with the potential benefits to the environment (as well as to your bottom line), there are likely to be government agencies enthusiastic to assist and tax-breaks for investments that reduce your carbon footprint.

80 UNDERSTAND WHAT YOU'RE GIVING AWAY

SOME CUSTOMERS 'GENEROUSLY' offer to come and help you take cost out of the products you make for them. Just be careful what you're getting into!

Look at how you agree on prices with your customer. Some will engage in a form of 'open book costing' where, for example, it may be agreed that they will pay the cost of materials and the cost of labour, plus an agreed % uplift to cover your other business costs and your profit margin.

But what happens when they help you find ways to reduce those material and labour costs?

The idea

If your customer offers to come and help you take cost out of their products, prepare your case and agenda carefully!

Potential suppliers of this automotive business are required to quote for business by setting out the amount of material to be used and the cost per unit of that material; the number of production hours required at a pre-determined hourly rate; an agreed % uplift to cover any other business costs; and an agreed profit margin. If successful, the quoted price becomes the agreed order price.

This can create quite a problem when the customer decides to help the supplier by using his purchasing power to enable them to reduce material costs by 10%.

	Quotation	Price after 'Cost Reduction' Activity	Cost after 'Cost Reduction' Activity
	£	£	£
Materials :			
100 kg @£10 per kilo	1,000		
@£8		800	800
Labour :			
5 hours @£40 per hour	200	200	200
Product Cost	1,200	1,000	1,000
Other Business Costs (33% Product Cost)	400	330	400
Total Costs	1,600	1,330	1,400
Profit margin (5% Total Cost)	80	70	
Selling price	£1,680	£1,400	

The supplier has agreed to a price that means he no longer makes a profit. It's that absorption costing problem again (see IDEA 26)!

Similar problems arise when you are helped to use less material and/ or fewer production hours. Just because you take material or labour costs out of the product doesn't mean those other costs disappear. Unless you can find ways to also reduce your other business costs (or fill that released capacity with additional profitable work) your profits will suffer. So you need to prepare for these visits.

Don't let them cherry-pick

If 'help' is offered, think about which products you're going to agree that the customer looks at. Remember product costs change throughout the demand life-cycle (see IDEA 64). Make sure that your customer doesn't just cherry-pick those products that you've already worked hard on to improve costs and are now running smoothly through the business (the 'cows').

You may well already be using less material now than you quoted and requiring less production time – but things will have been very different in the early stages of product introduction and are likely to deteriorate again when volumes fall. So include as many 'stars' and 'dogs' on the visit as you can.

Give and take

Talk to your people about aspects of the way you do business with this customer that cause hassle.

- Does the customer provide order schedules sufficiently far in advance – and are those schedules reliable?

- Do they issue materials for you to use and are these always delivered on time?

- Do they have to sign off completed orders before they are shipped – and is someone always available to do this?

- Do they provide the packaging – and is it there when you need it?

- Do they provide transportation – and does it arrive when it should?

- Do they pay your invoices on time?

If you can use these visits to resolve such matters, you can start to eliminate some of those other business costs – and if you're really smart, end up saving far more than you're having to give away!

In practice

- When quoting on an 'open book' basis, be careful to tie in quotes to order volumes – customers have a nasty habit of asking you to quote on a high volume of estimated annual call-off only for you to then find out that the actual volumes are significantly lower.

- If your customer offers you his 'help' in reducing your costs, think carefully about which products you want him to look at.

- Don't forget to prepare a list of all those 'hassle factors' and make sure they're also up for discussion so that you have the opportunity to claw back more than you may have to give away.

81. UNDERSTANDING THE MARKET

ALL YOU HAVE to do for business success is to meet market needs in the most cost-effective way... easy! Or perhaps not...

What is your business?

Are you sure?

The idea

Ask your customer what he is buying.

When you do you may be surprised to find that it isn't quite the same thing as what you think you are selling!

Do your sales team have a clear understanding of what existing and potential customers really want to buy – and successfully communicate this to those responsible for designing, manufacturing, delivering and servicing your offering to the market?

Do salespeople know the value customers place on having different needs met?

Sell solutions

As businesses and individuals (i.e. your customers) look to simplify their supply-chains, there is a demand for 'solutions not components'. Rather than purchasing a range of consumable items (such as tools or stationery) through a myriad of suppliers, many customers want a one-stop-shop where the customer not only delivers the complete range but also regularly replenishes stocks on a *kanban* system. (The word *kanban* translates as 'sign' and such systems signal when items need replenishing, thereby minimising the amount of inventory held.)

Other companies look to their suppliers to take a more active role in design.

Suppliers offering these kinds of solutions are saving their customers money. To be sustainable, the supplier must be able to organise his activities in a manner that allows him to make a living from the price the customer is willing to pay for the 'solution' offered (see IDEA 94).

It can prove profitable to look at how your customer uses your products...

The salesman from this parts manufacturer tracked his product through the processes in his customer's goods receiving area, and onwards into a kit marshalling stores area where it was duly booked into inventory. There it sat until a couple of minor parts were available from which the usable kit could be built. He saw his opportunity. For a profitable management fee he now buys those minor parts himself and sells his customer complete kits. The customer saves the time, space and inventory-holding costs of the marshalling activity by having the kits delivered directly to the production line ready for use.

In practice

- Look at your business through your customers' eyes.

- Take the opportunity to spot gaps in the market.

- Ask customers why they buy the products or services you offer – what precise needs are they seeking to meet?

- Don't just talk to existing customers – what about the ones whose needs you're not meeting?

82 UNLIKELY PARTNERS

AT A RAILWAY station it was interesting to see that a coffee shop was running a store within a store by allowing a major newspaper retailer vending space. Customers had a one-stop-shop for hot drinks and something to read, with the automated till sorting out the financials.

The idea

If you can't reduce your costs, try sharing them.

Sometimes you can find partners in unlikely places...

Beyond belief
An enterprising church-worker saw the opportunity to offer a service to local businesses while raising money towards necessary repair work to the church. One of her responsibilities was to have in place a team of volunteers who would post leaflets through every door in the parish to promote church activities. Local businesses were offered the opportunity to 'piggy-back' this service and have flyers delivered at the same time in return for a small donation to church funds. Of course, not all businesses were considered suitable...

Making room
Strapped for cash but still anxious to have the benefits of holding certain meetings 'off-site', this group got together with others in the neighbourhood to swap meeting rooms as and when required. Run on the same basis as a 'baby-sitting circle', members earn and use 'tokens' and can usually arrange catering if required for a small fee.

There are also some very unusual partnerships to be had if you look creatively at who might value things that you are currently paying to have taken off your hands (see IDEA 11).

In practice

- Look creatively for opportunities to share costs with other businesses.

  - If you are in manufacturing, could you share floorspace with either with your customer or your supplier (see IDEA 63)?

  - If you are in retailing, could you share floorspace with a business offering complementary products, thereby increasing footfall?

- Could you use collective buying power to attract bigger discounts on some purchases (e.g. stationery) or services (e.g. cleaning)? Take a look at IDEA 33.

WASTE NOT WANT NOT

IDENTIFYING WASTE STARTS with understanding what exactly the customer is buying from you – which may be surprisingly different from what you think you are selling (see IDEA 81).

Once you understand what gives your product or service 'value' in the eyes of the customer you are then in a position to understand 'waste' – or '*muda*' (the Japanese term for waste).

The idea

Waste is anything you do that does not add value (from the customer's perspective) to your product or service. Whenever we waste time or resources, it causes additional costs to the business that the customer will not value and therefore reduces profit.

Taiichi Ohno* of Toyota identified 7 categories of waste that are often described as:

- **Overproduction** – making more than is needed by the customer

- **Inventory** – holding excess materials in the system

- **Transport** – the unnecessary movement of materials

- **Movement** – people having to make unnecessary movements

- **Waiting** – working time not being used productively to add value

- **Inappropriate processes** – using inappropriate methods or tools

- **Defects** – producing scrap or work that has to be re-done

Dipping into the book, you can pick up some great ideas for identifying and eliminating all sorts of waste. Here are some to get you started:

Overproduction

This manufacturing company used to get round the problem of high scrap rates (another waste) by launching batches of 20 billets of raw material when the customer had ordered 17 finished parts. If they managed to make 18 nobody would update the system with the information that not only did they now already have one in stock; but also as they were now performing better, they could afford to reduce the number of billets launched next time.

Inappropriate processes

Working towards a manufacturing strategy of one-piece flow (i.e. batch sizes of one), this other business was thwarted by their six-spindle machine. This inappropriate process meant that pragmatically it was inevitable that stock would be held at both ends of the operation. Something for the to-do list when the opportunity came to replace the machine...

In practice

- Look critically at all aspects of your business. If you're not carrying out work that the customer values – or carrying it out in the most effective way – then you've got waste. And if you've got waste, you have an opportunity to improve your costs and increase your profits.

*   *Toyota Production System: Beyond Large-Scale Production*

WE'LL PUT THAT RIGHT LATER...

WHAT DO YOU do when a product fails test? Is there a tendency to set it on one side while you rush another one through the system to satisfy the customer? But if you keep doing this and no attention is paid to why this is happening...

The idea

Turning a blind eye in the hope that a problem will disappear is not an appropriate strategy if you want to manage costs.

Shelving the problem

Determined to understand why there was so much inventory in the business, this newly appointed manager examined the inventory valuation tabulation and asked for an explanation of the £300,000 against a code he did not recognise. Not satisfied with the shrugged response that 'it had been there for a long time', he dug deeper. Asking to physically view this inventory he was led to a cupboard on the shopfloor. The cupboard was stacked with cardboard boxes full of products that he discovered, on examination of the accompanying paperwork, had failed test and were waiting rework.

So why was nobody re-working them?

Why weren't customers screaming for their orders?

The answer to the second question was the easiest. Realising there was some kind of blockage in the system, instead of finding out what was going on, the planner just kept launching more and more orders to the shop in the hope of eventually enough coming out the other end to keep the customer happy.

As to why nobody was re-working them, it came down to a question of training and self-respect. The products that failed test were passed to an engineer for re-working. This engineer had been promoted into the position from the shopfloor but had not been trained adequately in how to systematically analyse test failures and re-work the product. When he was unable to resolve the problem quickly, fearful that his manager would think badly of him, rather than ask for help he would just open the cupboard door...

The solution? Let's go back to the fitter who was testing the product in the first place. Rather than just pass the unit on to the engineer when it fails test, he now works through a 'decision tree' analysis drawn up in conjunction with the engineering department to identify the cause of the failure and fixes it himself. A simple logging system allows information to be recorded and analysed on the reason for failures. Only if he is unable to fix it himself does he then pass it to an engineer for more in-depth analysis.

There are a great number of 'wins' here. It's not just a question of releasing the £300,000 investment tied up in inventory that wasn't going anywhere. The fitters take greater pride in their work and enjoy the challenge of being able to fix problems themselves. The logging system provides the information required for further root cause analysis to identify and eliminate the reasons for initial failures (see IDEA 27). Engineering time is released for more demanding technical work.

And the cupboard has been taken away.

In practice

- If there's a problem there's a cost attached to it, so you need to tackle problems rather than bury them – or they could end up burying you.

- In this instance the problem manifested itself as inventory. Remember that inventory doesn't just 'happen' – it's there for a reason. If you want to release the investment, you have to identify why it's there and then change the way you do things (see IDEA 96).

- Look for 'cupboards' in all your processes – and clear them out!

85 WHAT A DIFFERENCE A DAY MAKES

When setting out on that hazardous journey around the Working Capital cycle (see IDEA 40), it's important to understand not just where the destination is (your customer paying you) but also how to manage that final stage in an efficient and timely manner.

The idea

While it is often said that 'the customer comes first', it is not just a question of getting the goods to the customer on time, as you'll also be told that 'we all work for the customer'. So if you're working for him you need to make sure you're paid by him – at the earliest opportunity.

You've made the product and shipped it to your customer (or performed the service) and have raised any necessary paperwork and issued the invoice. How long will you have to wait to be paid?

It depends on the credit period you have negotiated with your customer and the timing of your invoice. (Of course it also depends on whether your customer is satisfied on matters such as quality and is going to honour the terms agreed. If you're interested in ways to improve your hit-rate at collecting money on time and avoiding overdues, take a look at IDEAS 28 & 95.)

Credit terms

When entering sales negotiations it is important to consider not just what the customer is going to pay but also when he is going to pay.

In planning cashflow you need to be crystal clear on the contractual payment terms agreed with your customer. These terms usually relate to the invoice date – but remember that in most instances you are not allowed to invoice until the goods have been shipped! If you have agreed 'Net 30' terms you can expect payment 30 days after the invoice date. If, however, the terms are 'Net monthly account' you would have to wait until the last day of the month following the one in which the invoice is dated. So if goods due to be shipped on 31st March do not leave until 1st April (or even more frustratingly if the goods leave as planned but the invoice doesn't get raised until the following day)...

Critical dates
Missing a month-end deadline by one day could mean an extra month waiting for payment – and it is unlikely that employees or suppliers will be willing to wait an extra month to be paid.

Missing reserved space on a container ship may prove even more costly.

A delay in being able to invoice might not be down to someone on your payroll...

Regain control
The products made by this manufacturer had to be signed off for quality by the customer's inspector before invoicing. As the inspector had to come from overseas, he was reluctant to travel unless there were a number of units to be inspected. In bad weather he wouldn't come at all. Frustrated by their inability to trigger invoicing, the manufacturer delved back into the records to find out when and why this process had started.

He established that many years ago there had been a problem of poor quality and a high level of rejects on receipt by the customer so the procedure had been put in place as a 'fix'. (It was never a proper 'fix' was it? Just a pragmatic short-term response to get round a problem while the quality issue was being properly and permanently resolved. If there was no longer a problem with quality...)

The manufacturer gathered evidence that the improvement in their quality standards was such as to no longer necessitate this procedure. The source inspector now signs off the units by fax after scrutinising the internally-generated inspection reports, enabling the manufacturer to get on with invoicing for the work he has done.

In practice

- Make sure your sales team are clear on the cost to the business of allowing customers credit and understand this is a vital aspect of their negotiations.

- Ensure there is clarity of understanding between all parties on agreed credit terms.

- Consider the credit terms when setting shipment or delivery dates – and check that people working in despatch understand the significance of these dates when juggling transportation arrangements (see IDEA 93).

86 WHAT DID BIG BEN SAY TO THE LEANING TOWER OF PISA?

"I'VE GOT THE time if you've got the inclination."

The idea

Getting hooked on finding ways to do more with less often starts in a small way.

Room for improvement

At a recent seminar, a delegate from overseas spoke of how he had been able to book a low-cost flight to the venue but was then aggrieved by the quoted cost for his hotel room for one night – three times the cost of his return flight. Although he was looking to make a booking a week or so in advance, he turned his attention to internet sites offering 'last-minute' discounts and was able to book the same room in the same hotel for the same night for half the cost. His advice? A minute can last longer than you might think. His motivation? A refusal to accept the relative costs of flight and accommodation. It would be interesting to know whether he would have sought a better price for his hotel room had the flight been more expensive...

Time for change

Like many people, this manager of a long-established engineering company was having difficulty gaining momentum to much-needed improvement activities in his business. The principle excuse proferred? "I just haven't got the time to get involved." Knowing that all too often the reason for this lack of time is the very reason for the need for improvements (repeated short-term fixes for recurring problems), the manager decreed that one hour per working week was to be set aside for those participating in teams to tackle 'low hanging fruit' (quick, easy-win activities). Fired-up by their successes (and the beneficial effect on workload pressures), enthusiasm for joining teams and finding the next 'win' grew. Now 50% of the workforce are actively involved in improvement activities and the percentage is growing...

Feed on success

This manager had the foresight to realise there was an opportunity to harness the under-utilised capabilities of his and other senior managers' personal assistants (PAs). When he first asked them to work as a team to review catering on the site and come back with their recommendations, there was some reticence as the PAs were not used to stepping outside their departmental comfort-zones. A few weeks later, however, the team presented their findings with some great ideas of how to organise things better while reducing costs. Fired up with a sense of achievement, enhanced job satisfaction and a better understanding of other parts of the business, they couldn't wait to tackle their next project, the telephone system...

(If you want some of their ideas on catering take a look at IDEA 45.)

In practice

- Like yoghurt, it's all down to culture.

- If you face negativity, take a look at IDEA 91 for help in preparing a convincing argument for improving costs.

- Cost improvement activities are addictive but you need to find a way to get people hooked. It's worth working on your 'carriers' – those key people who have disproportionate influence on behavioural norms and attitudes to work (see IDEA 51).

87 WHAT'S THIS WORTH TO YOU?

ACTIVITIES CAUSE COST. If you do something there is a cost attached to it, so it makes sense to improve your costs by eliminating activities that nobody wants.

But how about activities that are required?

Do your internal customers know what your products, services or information cost to produce? Is the price (i.e. cost) worth it? Is there a more cost-effective way of achieving the same outcome?

The idea

Look for opportunities to simplify and streamline processes to save time – and therefore money.

Flushed with success at eliminating the activities involved in making 'products' for which there were no customers, the lecturer we met in IDEA 23 now turned his attention to the stack of paper forms that were currently issued by various departments to every new student. Each form had to be signed and then returned (probably the trickiest bit!) to be filed away for future reference by the appropriate end-user.

Looking for a win-win outcome, the lecturer also happened to be spearheading a campaign to make sure students made early contact with their tutors, who would be better-positioned to spot the symptoms of academic derailment all too common in new undergraduates. Every student is now required to meet their tutor within the first few days of term and, during this meeting, signs one piece of paper on which all the required authorisations are listed.

Now the administrators just have the tutors to chase!

In practice

- Look at how you can work together with your internal suppliers, your department, and your customers to re-engineer processes to make them more cost-effective.

- List the outputs (products, services or information) you produce for internal customers and start with the ones that cause you most hassle. Because hassle means cost.

- After checking that you're producing something your customer values, question just how much he values it! Work out a rough cost of producing the information and ask your customer – if they had to carry the cost on their budget, would they buy it?

88 WHEN THINGS GO WRONG

NURTURE AND CHERISH good relationships with your customers as it's usually far cheaper to continue to sell to your existing customers, than to have to carry out the necessary investment to win new ones.

The idea

If you want value from your advertising, sales and marketing costs, remember the importance of customer loyalty. So you need to work at building and maintaining good customer relationships – but not at any cost!

What can you do when things go wrong?

Beware the free-lunchers
You do need to be sure something *has* gone wrong. Not all people are as honest as you might hope. A restaurateur found to his cost that it soon became common knowledge that if a diner complained about some aspect of their meal (whether they had finished it or not) the manager would unhesitatingly remove the cost from the final bill.

Money straight off the bottom line. Perhaps he was courting loyalty from the wrong clientele.

If something genuinely goes wrong, how can you come out of the situation looking good?

Lost baggage – not lost reputations
Strangely, airlines seem to be able to do this. If bags are lost in transit but re-united with their owners with impressive speed and efficiency, this is frequently used as a reason for recommending the airline to other travellers!

(One bank used to take the idea of coming out 'smelling of roses' literally and would send out floral gifts to appease irate customers. Perhaps it would have been a good idea to monitor how many bouquets had gone to the same address and turn their attentions to fixing the problem rather than keeping the local florist afloat.)

Whatever you do will cost money. So you don't just keep on forking out over and over again... do you?

If at first you don't succeed...

A customer wanted to buy a cheap desk for her young daughter's bedroom. She found a self-assembly one that came as three separate parts (a top, a leg and a cupboard) for under £20. When she got home she unwrapped the packages and found that the top of the desk was badly damaged at the edge. She phoned the store and they promised to deliver a replacement – a round-trip for them of 80 miles. When the replacement arrived it too was damaged and the driver took it back. The same thing happened again. Eventually one arrived in an acceptable condition. Did anyone ever pick up on the customer's suggestion that it would have saved the company a fortune in delivery costs if they had just checked the condition of the desk top before they set out? Or much better still, fixed the packaging to provide sufficient protection down each edge?

In practice

- Recognise that every £1 that has to be spent 'putting things right' for your customer is £1 straight off the bottom line, so make sure that the cause of the problem is identified and fixed – permanently (see IDEA 27).

- If products do have to be returned to you under warranty, don't forget to manage the cost of freight (see IDEA 93).

89
WHERE SHOULD WE MAKE THIS?

Don't end up paying someone else's overheads as well as your own!

Costing systems should come with a health warning and you should check how yours is compiled before using it to help you make decisions.

The idea

When tackling 'make-buy' decisions, remember to look beyond your costing system.

Moving work out to a sub-contractor who can do an operation in the same time that it takes you but charges a lower hourly rate may end up costing you more. Why?

Absorption costing uses a 'burden rate' to charge out business costs to products – see IDEA 26. The rate therefore 'recovers' costs including supervisory and managerial salaries, rent and rates, travel costs, advertising etc. Products 'absorb' the business costs by the application of this rate to, typically, the number of hours the product requires in production.

Just because you move an hour's worth of work out to a sub-contractor doesn't necessarily mean you save money.

Example

Assume your cost-rate is £80 per hour. A product currently made in-house takes an hour in production and thus picks up £80 of business costs. Your sub-contractor's rate is £60. How much do you save if you sub-contract out that hour's worth of work? It depends on what you are going to do with the hour of spare capacity you have now created in production. Moving work (and hence hours) doesn't mean £80 of your costs disappear for every hour you re-route. If you've nothing productive to fill the spare hour with (i.e. work that a customer will pay for), then most of your £80 costs will still be there – and now you're paying £60 of your sub-contractor's business costs as well.

And the problem doesn't stop there.

The increased handling of the product as it moves on- and off-site may well lead to increased scrap (see IDEA 41).

You also need to consider all those additional transportation, supplier qualification, purchasing costs, receiving and administrative costs you'll incur. If moving work out increases your inventory, there are the interest costs to consider and the increase in your risk exposure (see IDEA 6).

If your stock is valuable, there will be the cost of safeguarding it.

Physical separation between you and your sub-contractor may bring communication challenges and when there's a problem it may be harder and take longer to resolve.

[These issues can be exacerbated when dealing with manufacture in other countries. Don't overlook the cost of the support required in terms of travel costs (the impact of a reduction in time spent locally as well as the travel expenses) and expat salary expectations.]

Strategic factors
There are strategic reasons for manufacturing in certain locations – e.g. to open up new markets.

There are strategic reasons not to outsource certain manufacturing processes – e.g. development of an eventual competitor.

Financial evaluation
The financial input to the decision should be evaluated on an

incremental cost basis. What additional costs will you incur if you move the work elsewhere compared to the savings you will make by no longer having the work on-site? Note that you are likely to have a different answer depending on the timescale under consideration ,as while you may be unable to use any freed-up space and capacity in the short-term, they may have great value to you in the longer term – e.g. to position you for taking on a new product line.

There can sometimes be an unexpected twist to the decision to move to 'low-cost economy' suppliers.

An engineering business in the USA was buying 20,000 coils per annum from a local supplier who charged $12 each. The item was re-sourced overseas to a 'low-cost economy', reducing the cost to $7. Initially the quality was great but eventually began to deteriorate. The original supplier was contacted and asked if he would like to regain the business on a dual-supplier basis on condition that he matched the $7 price. Keen to regain the work and having been spurred into cost improvement action by losing the order in the first place, the original supplier took the business offered. As the quality from the overseas supplier continued to deteriorate, all supplies now come from the original supplier – but at a much-reduced price.

In practice

- Talk to those involved in 'make-buy' decisions and look at the basis being used to assess financial impact.

- Compile a 'check-list' in the form of a template covering the types of incremental costs and benefits relevant to your business in 'make-buy' decisions.

- Note that if your business gets overly enthusiastic in putting work out, you could inadvertently enter the death spiral... (see IDEA 73)

90

WHERE THERE'S A PROBLEM THERE'S A COST

IF YOU WANT to run a cost-efficient business, you need to be able to complete the Working Capital cycle (from cash back into cash again) as fast as you can and with minimum effort.

WORKING CAPITAL CYCLE

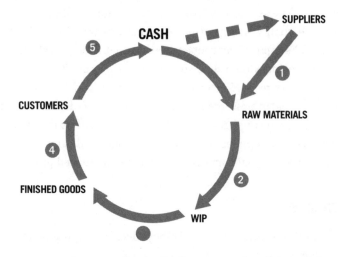

(For more information on the Working Capital cycle see IDEA 40.)

The idea

Every time you deviate from the shortest, most efficient, route to your destination on the working Working Capital cycle (your customer paying you for what you've done), you've wasted time and money.

Wherever there's a problem on the journey there is a cost. And that journey is extremely hazardous with loads of opportunity for getting it wrong.

In fact when you think about it, it's amazing you ever complete the journey 'right first time'!

Do you ever buy the wrong things from your suppliers? If you do, and you have to scrap the stuff off, you may as well have just sat in the corner of the office dropping £50 notes into the shredding machine.

Do you ever bring in temporary labour who may not have been adequately trained and then end up rejecting goods? More work for the shredding machine.

Do you ever get your materials and your labour right, but having failed to maintain your equipment properly end up producing scrap? The shredding machine awaits.

Do you get your materials, your labour and your equipment right but find out that you didn't quite understand the customer's specification...

The possibilities are endless. As are the opportunities to improve.

In practice

- Learn to recognise when people are dropping £50 notes into the shredder – obvious examples include scrap and where work has to be re-done.

- If you look carefully you will find people beavering away spending their entire working lives at the shredder – because they are employed to 'cover up' an imperfect process or carry out unnecessary tasks.

- Get rid of the shredder by getting to the root cause of problems and then fixing them – permanently (see IDEA 27).

WHET APPETITES!

ANNOUNCEMENTS OF CAMPAIGNS to improve costs can often be greeted by groans and a noticeable lack of enthusiasm.

Even when your back is against the wall and you need to find savings to be able to requote more competitive prices to keep existing business or prevent work moving to another location, initial reactions may be disappointing. "What's the point?" "It's not going to make much difference."

Muttered comments recall eras when employees had to hand over pencil stubs before they got a new one... and bring their own cutlery to work to reduce canteen costs. (Surprisingly this last one is not a corporate myth.)

The idea

When faced with negativity, demonstrate the impact a small percentage reduction in costs can have.

Take a look at this...
If your company currently makes a profit of £2,000 and you cut costs by 2% how much would your profits increase by? £400? (i.e. 2%)

No! If things are pretty tight they could double!

	Current position	After saving 2% costs
	£	£
Sales	100,000	Sales 100,000
Costs	98,000	Costs 96,000
	————————	————————
Profit	2,000	4,000

Think about what cost savings of 4%, 5% or possibly 10% would do!

Having grabbed peoples' attention, now reel them in. Explain that this isn't something a few managers can do on their behalf. There is a huge wealth of talent, experience and ideas held by everyone in the workforce and this needs to be harnessed if the business is to put in a winning performance.

Few individuals can have the knowledge to win '*Who wants to be a Millionaire?*' – but put together the right team and you have a much better chance (as one contestant found out to his initial advantage but, once judged to have cheated, to his ultimate cost).

In practice

- Work out the impact on profit of incremental cost savings in your business and make sure everyone knows the scale of the opportunity.

- Explain that profit is not a dirty word! Profits provide the business with the cheapest and least risky form of finance for investing in the new products, services and facilities that are needed in order to compete and survive.

- Then check out some of the other IDEAS to kickstart the cost improvement process.

92 WHO IS YOUR COST CZAR?

How CAN YOU improve your costs if you don't understand them? Someone in your organisation needs to be an expert.

The idea

If you look at your business it's easy (if you keep decent records) to know to the penny what you spend – just look at the invoices you receive and your payroll. The problem is identifying which resources are used for the activities you undertake in delivering each of the products or services to your customers.

Enter your cost czar.

Who does what?
In businesses there are two types of accountants: financial accountants and management accountants.

Large organisations may have separate departments; smaller organisations may have schizophrenic accountants who undertake both roles; in small businesses both roles may be merely a subset of the various hats worn by the boss.

Financial accountants 'do the books'. After all someone has to do them for tax purposes and to meet legal reporting requirements. But management accounting is a service – the purpose is to collect, analyse, interpret and communicate information on costs to allow the rest of the workforce to make better decisions.

Mirror reality

When running an in-house financial awareness course in the subsidiary of a large multi-national organisation, this client asked for advice on prioritising the initial workload for the newly appointed management accountant who was arriving the following week. Frankly, in terms of understanding costs, the business was a shambles. Expecting a response of 'Budgeting' or 'Costing', the question put to the client was obviously surprising.

"Will they have an office?" On finding they would, the answer was easy.

"Lock their office door before they arrive and don't let them in for at least two weeks!"

Every business is unique. Cost information should 'mirror the reality' of what is going on. No two businesses bring in the same resources, do the same things to them and produce the same outputs. Therefore until you understand how resources (and hence costs) come into, move through and leave the business you cannot produce meaningful information.

The new appointee had a lot of walking, talking and watching to do before they would be of any value to the business.

(This particular example happened some years ago before the advent of the open-plan office. These days you could achieve the same result by taking away their chair for a while.)

In practice

- Get to know the person who puts together cost information in your business – if you don't know who they are, that suggests there's even more opportunity to improve matters!

- Arrange to walk them through your department (and encourage others to do the same). Talk about the skills required of the people you employ and the equipment and services you use. Explain the activities you undertake and what you produce (including products, services and information) for internal and/or external customers. Tell them your problems. After all, where there's a problem there's a cost (see IDEA 90).

- Note that however well you and your colleagues have enlightened your cost czar, all product costing involves an element of 'professional judgement' – so don't believe everything you read (see IDEA 26)!

93 WHO PAYS THE FERRYMAN?

IF THE CUSTOMER has placed an order, he's expecting to receive the goods.

But whose responsibility is it to deliver them? Whose liability is it if they are lost or damaged in transit?

Your answers to these questions has an important impact on the profit margins you're going to make.

The idea

When negotiating contracts with customers, make sure you understand where the responsibility for freight and insurance lie and if it's with you, that you look for cost-effective solutions.

Try to consolidate shipments, but remember...

Time is money
Check out those credit terms the customer has negotiated. When does the clock start ticking? Will this influence your mode of transport?

Do despatch have an up-to-date production schedule of what's heading their way and customer requirement dates?

Has anyone explained to them what a difference a day might make in payment terms (see IDEA 85)?

Does your despatch department have a hockey-stick (see IDEA 22)?

Stamp out waste
Could documents be emailed rather than posted?

Who selects which postal service should be used?

Are the factors that affect cost such as size and weight understood?

Who co-ordinates courier services?

Marginal improvement
Where you can reclaim freight costs, have you negotiated discounts with carriers but quoted your customer the full amount?

Do you reclaim the cost of freighting rejected goods back to suppliers?

Who checks that you don't end up paying the inward freight for reworked goods twice?

If you have to pay for goods to come back in under warranty, either organise collection when your trucks are running empty or, where possible, specify the carrier to be used.

Look for opportunities to hitch a ride...

Transport surveys have suggested that 25% trucks are running empty and 50% are partially loaded. Look for websites where there are reverse auctions for transportation needs. You specify what you need to move and where it needs to go to and from, and then your request will be matched to hauliers with capacity to suit.

Worth considering.

In practice

Your supply chain has links.

- Make sure there is clarity about where the logistical and financial responsibility lies for passing goods on.

- Your planning schedules should allow you to make cost-effective shipping choices without compromising on-time delivery. If you have problems with schedule adherence, identify the root causes and deal with them – or else resign yourself to chucking wads of £50 notes into the shredder in despatch.

- Take a look at what you're shipping and how it's packed. There may be great opportunities to improve your freight costs by working with packaging suppliers and hauliers to understand shipping constraints.

- If you are engaged in international trade make sure you avoid misunderstandings by using Incoterms (e.g. FCA, FOB, CIF) – and that you understand the cost implications you may be literally taking onboard!

94 WHO SETS THE SELLING PRICE?

FOR THE VAST majority of businesses, the market sets the selling price for the product or service you have chosen to offer. You try to position yourself so that you can maximise the price you can charge (and still win the business) by being the one the customer prefers to buy from – because of your great quality, service, relationships, etc.

The idea

Everyone knows that Selling price – Costs = Profit.

So if the price is set by the market, does that mean you shrug your shoulders and abdicate responsibility for how much profit your business makes?

Of course you don't. You manage your costs.

It is important to start by understanding precisely what your customer is buying from you (see IDEA 81). Having established this, your task is now to align your business to meet those market needs in the most cost-effective way. Just as the market will not reward you for providing features of a product or service that it doesn't value, neither will it pay you a premium just because you have chosen to make it or deliver it inefficiently. In some instances, this requires a massive shift in culture.

For many years, defence contracts were negotiated on a cost-plus basis, with the selling price being determined by what the product cost to make plus an agreed percentage for profit.

Questionably not the most effective use of taxpayers' money, as of course the higher the supplier's costs, the greater the profit they made.

Nor a great incentive for supplier cost-control!

Businesses unused to having to foot the bill for the cost of their inefficiencies have been rudely awakened by the advent of competitive tendering and, even more of a challenge, cost-down contracts where they are committed to make year-on-year reductions in price.

There's only one way to reduce prices and still maintain profit margins – and that's to improve costs.

Now there's an incentive!

In practice

- Look at your offerings through your customers' eyes and make sure you understand what gives your products or services value.

- Having eliminated the cost of providing features that your customer doesn't need, look to how you provide those valued characteristics in the most cost-effective way by eliminating waste.

- Don't worry – there are 99 other ideas in the book to get you started!

95

WHY DON'T THEY JUST PAY UP?

WHOSE JOB IS it to collect the cash? Is it just the responsibility of those working in accounts receivable?

No.

There is only one person who brings cash into the business – the customer. It's frustrating (and costly) enough that you have to wait for your money throughout the negotiated credit period.

But if customers still don't pay...

Shouldn't you be turning your attentions to collecting those debts?

Overdues mean tying up even more money in Working Capital resulting in additional borrowing and hence higher interest costs.

If customers do not pay up, you may run out of cash and have no business left.

The longer a debt is unpaid, the increased likelihood of it going 'bad' and you being unable to collect it at all. All that work for nothing and all that money in the shredding machine (see IDEA 90).

Now convinced you need to act?

The idea

If you are having problems getting customers to pay on time, don't just rant and rave about them 'being difficult' and 'messing you around', dig down and find the root cause.

There are a myriad of reasons why customers do not pay on time and few are down to lackadaisical accounts receivable personnel.

Doing a 'causal analysis' of your overdue debts may reveal instances of:

- Lack of agreement on the credit period negotiated

- Customers not having received the invoice because it was sent to the wrong address

- Problems with the invoice:

  - incorrect part numbers

  - incorrect quantities

  - no order number quoted – perhaps because no customer order was raised

  - prices not in agreement with the order

- Goods delivered to the wrong place

- No evidence of goods being received

- Damaged goods or faulty services

- Goods not fit for the purpose the customer intended

- Incorrect packaging

- Documentation missing (warranties, service manuals etc.)

Once you know why there's a problem, you then need to dig out those root causes to stop the problem happening again (see IDEA 27).

It has been known for overdues to be down to your customer's administrative chaos...

Costing the earth

This manufacturer of earth-moving equipment found getting money from their main customer a nightmare and had a small team of people dedicated to the task. Goods would have been delivered and approved, but the customer seemed unable to complete their own paper-chase culminating in payment.

The supplier spotted an opportunity. His customer was a nationalised industry on the verge of privatisation where the main concern was showing purchasing savings rather than cashflow. In return for a small discount on price, it was agreed that invoices would be paid automatically by bank transfer 15 days after submission, and then the customer would have 30 days in which to raise queries regarding the payments made. The manufacturer got his cash promptly (substantially reducing the amount tied up in Working Capital) and, by filling existing vacancies, could re-deploy the team of credit controllers elsewhere in the business. Giving away the discount proved a price well worth paying!

In practice

- Carry out a causal analysis on overdue debts and use the information to root out problems to prevent them taking hold and choking off access to your cash.

- Prevention is the best policy. Manage your receivables so that you have the opportunity to iron out any problems with invoices well before the due date – see IDEA 28.

96 WHY IS THAT INVENTORY HERE?

BEWARE QUACKS!

If you're looking to reduce your investment in inventory, watch out for rogue consultants working on commission who will hang around just long enough to take their cut as inventory levels are reduced and inventory values fall – but who will have disappeared into thin air when, inevitably, a few months later, you find it's all come back again.

Boomerang inventory.

Inventory does not just happen, it's there for a reason. Inventory is the consequence of the way you've chosen to organise your business.

The idea

If you want to get rid of inventory, you have to understand why it's there (the cause) and then change the way you do things so that the inventory is no longer required.

Answering these questions might provide a starting point.

Is the lead time for products greater than the lead time required by the customer when he places an order? If so, you'll have to hold inventory if you're going to deliver on time.

Do your customers insist on you holding inventory on consignment (often on their premises) because of previous poor delivery adherence (see IDEA 6)?

Do you end up holding buffer inventory because of unreliable suppliers (see IDEA 18)?

How much of the production lead time does your product spend having value added to it – and how much time does it spend hanging around in a queue at an operational bottleneck, or on the back of a lorry going to and from sub-contractors (see IDEA 41)?

Do your products take longer to complete their journey through the production process because they have to take a detour round the concession loop (see IDEA 53)?

Are you using an appropriate process? If you're producing one-off components for spares, you don't want to be using a 6 spindle machine. (see IDEA 47).

Are you buying parts when you could be buying kits? If you can't use parts until the kits are complete you have wads of money sitting on the shelf in your stores (see IDEA 81).

Motivated by quantity discounts, do you buy more materials than you need (see IDEA 30)?

Perhaps it's a question of who (or what) is in control.

There's no smoke...
Month after month there it sat propped against the wall in the stores gathering dust; the biggest marine component this business had ever made. (Let's call it a funnel.) With the customer having cancelled the order, it seemed nobody wanted to buy it but the manager was reluctant to scrap it off. Eventually a buyer was found, albeit for a knock-down price. A few weeks later the manager was astounded to find the funnel still in the stores. On enquiry he found out that the original funnel had indeed been sold but the MRP system, having recorded the sale, had automatically launched the order to replace the item...

There's another great example of how inventory 'happens' in IDEA 84 involving inadequate training, a misplaced concept of expectations and a conveniently large cupboard...

In practice

- Do a causal analysis of your own inventory.

- Remind yourself what a prominent role designers can play in determining how much inventory you're going to have to hold (see IDEA 97)!

  (If you need to remind yourself why you want to get rid of inventory, take a look at IDEA 37.)

97 YOU CAN READ IT IN THE STARS

If you don't get the design right you will pay the price.

And this is not about whether the final product is fit for purpose (although of course that is very important too and very costly should you get it wrong).

Whatever your business, the impact of the design decision on the financial outcome should be of concern to you. If your product has a long demand life-cycle that you will be contractually committed to supporting (e.g. through spares), this should be of great concern to you. If you have issues such as certification that mean it is prohibitively costly to change your design during this life-cycle, you should be even more concerned. As the designer lifts his pencil to the paper he may well be determining your company's profitability for many years into the future – or signing its death warrant.

The idea

Designers have a key role to play in ensuring you have a financially sustainable business, so it is really important to get them involved and make sure they understand the implications of the choices they make (see IDEA 39).

The way a product or service is designed will have a significant impact not only on what it costs in terms of labour and materials, but also on how much investment the company requires in Fixed Assets and Working Capital. The higher the investment, the more the company will have to rely on borrowed money and hence higher the cost of interest and the greater the financial risk.

Material impacts

Design drives the specification of the materials required and you need to think beyond just matters of price. For instance:

The materials specified constrain your selection of possible suppliers.

- How many alternative sources of supply are there?

- How much negotiating power do you have with them – not just in terms of price, but importantly, in continuity of delivery in times of short supply?

- Where are they geographically located? – as this will influence transportation costs, lead times, and hence the debate on the need for buffer stocks.

Method matters

An integral part of product design is the question of how it is to be made. Matters affecting cost and investment include:

- Can and should you make it in-house or should you sub-contract out all or part of the process?

- Is existing equipment and tooling appropriate for making this product in this way?

- How long will the product take to make? If it is longer than the lead-time required by the customer, you will have to lay down stock.

Further food for thought...

How easy is the product to make?

How steep a learning curve is there to go through?

The chances are your costing system will substantially understate the cost you incur as you go through this learning curve (see IDEA 26).

If you took into account how much it really costs to get a product up and running, would you have been prepared to spend a little more time and money up-front getting the design right?

In practice

- Talk to your designers about how their decisions impact the financial viability of the business (see IDEA 39).

- Make sure your designers don't dwell in some ivory tower away from the business realities of the consequences of their choices. In particular, check there are effective systems in place to feed information back to designers so that they don't repeat expensive mistakes.

- Note that most costing systems understate the real cost of launching new products – which means there are great opportunities to improve costs as, chances are, things are actually much worse than they appear!

98 YOU MAY HAVE SAVED TIME... BUT HAVE YOU SAVED ANY MONEY?

COSTING SYSTEMS should come with a health warning – check yours before using it for making decisions as it may well not be fit for this purpose.

IDEA 26 explains how absorption costing uses a 'burden rate' to charge out business costs to products. This is typically at an hourly rate based on how many hours the product requires in production. The rate therefore 'recovers' business costs including supervisory and managerial salaries, rent and rates, travel costs, advertising...

Be careful. Just because you take an hour out of the time required to make your product doesn't necessarily save you any money. Investing in tooling to reduce the time it takes to carry out a process could end up costing you more money if the time you release can't be used productively doing work that the customer will pay for.

The idea

Understand the potential for disagreements on quantifying the 'savings' made through improvement activities and develop a reporting format to motivate desired behaviours.

Let's start by looking at how accountants and those involved in cost improvement activities can end up at loggerheads.

Too good to be true

The Group Accountant of this multinational organisation was perplexed. He had been asked to report on the savings made throughout the group as a result of cost improvement activities. Having received this information from each of the subsidiaries, he found that when he totalled it up it exceeded the total profit for the group. Something didn't add up...

The old accounting-for-capacity problem.

Take the example of a simple cost improvement activity. Assume your cost-rate is £80 per hour. A product currently made in-house takes 6 hours in production and thus picks up £480 of business costs. If you can reduce the cycle-time by one hour, how much cost saving have you made?

That depends on what you are going to do with the hour of spare capacity you have now created in production. Reducing layout times doesn't mean £80 of your costs disappears for every hour worth of work you eliminate. If you've nothing productive to fill the spare time with (i.e. work that a customer will pay for), then most of your original costs will still be there (you'll possibly save a small amount on utilities, consumables etc.) and bizarrely, according to most costing systems, the cost of your other products goes up!

(If the business costs are still there but the hours to absorb them have gone down, the burden rate goes up, pushing up the cost of all the products you make. What nonsense!)

Our Group Accountant's problem was that the improvement teams had claimed to have saved the equivalent of £80 for every hour taken off manufacturing times and similarly over-estimated the savings from moving work to sub-contractors or 'low-cost' economies (see IDEA 89).

Come back!
But don't just shrug your shoulders and walk away. There is a serious issue here.

(Not least because it can cause a rift between those involved in improvement activities and accountants, when the former are told that there is no evidence of any benefit from all their efforts. Angry conversations ensue with claims and counter-claims about whose figures are correct... what a waste!)

But if the business can't immediately find the benefit of some of the activities 'on the bottom line', what's the point in doing them?

Because they're what I refer to as 'enablers'.

Follow through

Enablers are opportunities in disguise – and costly to ignore.

While managing expectations (see IDEA 50), you need to motivate teams to keep generating improvements whether they produce benefits immediately or whether, as enablers, they require 'following through' with a second step before those benefits can be realised.

By freeing up time (or indeed space – see IDEA 63), you are creating the opportunity to do something with it. You may not have that additional workload immediately, or be able to sub-let the space, but the cost of holding this opportunity needs to be reported separately in bright flashing lights, rather than spread thinly over the cost of all the products running through the business.

In practice

- Look at how you value and report on cost improvements in your business.

- Understand the opportunities presented by 'enablers' and highlight the cost of holding them by reporting them separately (see IDEA 50).

- Have a look at some of the other examples of how inappropriate use of costing 'information' can lead to products being made in the wrong place and a ride down the death spiral – see IDEAS 73 & 89.

99 YOU TELL ME WHAT WE NEED TO DO!

THERE IS A wealth of experience and talent in the workforce that all too often gets overlooked. If improvement activities are left to managers then the business is missing a huge opportunity.

The idea

Don't leave most of your players sitting on the bench.

Even when you're looking at the 'big picture' rather than telling people what needs to be done in terms of reducing costs and improving efficiency, it may be helpful to give them an opportunity to work it out for themselves.

An uncanny resemblance

This large manufacturing company in the metals sector had just run a series of financial awareness courses for managers from across the business. The trainer was then asked to repeat the sessions for the trade union representatives. It was thought it would be helpful to improve their basic financial understanding in preparation for a meeting with management to discuss steps to resolve poor profit performance and perpetual shortages of cash.

Rather than repeating the earlier sessions, the trainer adopted a different approach. Delegates were given the opportunity to 'buy' a business that they could 'run' using 'money' to purchase materials, turn them into products and then ship them out to customers. After taking a look at how the business worked, the delegates accepted the offer to buy and, as the new owners, set about their work. As they re-enacted one financial year after another, our new capitalists became increasingly frustrated by the lack of any return on their investment and muttered threats about closing the business down and moving on could be heard. Then the penny dropped – the business they were 'running' was a mirror image of the company they worked for. Understanding why there was a need to act, the delegates started to come up with their own ideas for improving performance... that bore a remarkable resemblance to the agenda for their forthcoming meeting.

In practice

- Recognise that relying on a small proportion of the workforce for ideas is wasting a great opportunity.

- If you want your co-workers to embrace change and join the fight against waste you have to lead from the front and be convincing about the benefits on offer (see IDEA 91)... and the risks of lagging behind your competition.

- Remember that many will ask "What's in it for me?" – so make sure you have your answers ready!

YOU'RE NOT STOPPING ARE YOU?

100

CONTINUOUS IMPROVEMENT... THE clue is in the name!

If you can really motivate those around you to get involved with identifying where the business is wasting money, attitudes change and the process becomes part of the culture... and positively addictive.

And the great news is that there are endless opportunities to get that buzz from finding ways to do more with less.

The idea

As discussed in IDEAS 81 & 94, for businesses to survive they must continuously seek to realign themselves to meet the needs of ever-changing markets. Not only that, but when there are changes earlier on in the supply chain, or changes in technology, or opportunities created by improvements made elsewhere in the business, it is time to question and challenge whether previous 'fixes' still offer the best solution.

Remember our lecturer from IDEA 23? He was surprised to find that in some quarters there was an initial reticence to stop producing the CDs for students. On investigation he found out that putting the information on CDs had been initiated a few years earlier as a huge improvement on an extremely wasteful paper process. It had been a 'great idea' of its time – but with the advent of wifi and students' ability to access the internet (and hence the up-to-date websites) even when they were on the move, there was now an even better solution... what next?

In practice

- Make sure that even the greatest ideas are not seen as 'the final solution' but 'of their time'.

- Retread old ground to see if you can now find even smarter ways of doing things.

- Look out for opportunities to get the improvement ripple effect – the ability to take a great idea generated in one part of the business and adapt it for use elsewhere.

  And...

- If you think you're finished, you've missed the point!

EXPLANATION OF TERMS

Investment

Fixed Assets – the investment in facilities and processes such as land, buildings, plant and equipment.

Working Capital – the investment in cash, inventory and net credit. i.e. **Cash + Inventory + (Receivables – Payables)**

Inventory (or Stock) – the sum of money invested in raw materials, work-in-progress and finished goods

Receivables (or Debtors) – the amount you are owed from your customers.

Payables (or Creditors) – the amount you owe your suppliers

Working Capital Cycle – The cycle of cash through the business back into cash again as customers pay for the products or services you have delivered (see IDEA 40).

Costing

Absorption Costing is a costing method in which business costs are 'absorbed' and charged out to products or services on the back of the labour hours or machine hours required using a **burden rate** (also known as a **cost rate**) (see IDEA 26).

Direct materials are the purchased materials that form part of the product or service you are selling.

Direct labour are the people (or payroll costs of the people) who work on the product you are selling, or who deliver the service you are performing.